Running for My Life,
The Diary of Alexis Love

Alexis Love

ISBN: 1984069136
ISBN-13: 978-1984069139

DEDICATION

This book is dedicated to God, the one who created me and gave me a second chance at life. I also dedicate this book to every woman, man and child who is running for their life.

CONTENTS

Part I: Recognizing the Giant

Part II: Use your Weapons

Part III: Victory is Yours

Alexis Love

FOREWORD

To the reader of this work:

From sending an email, to standing court-side with me at the Amway Center – home of the NBA's Orlando Magic – Alexis showed just how passionate she was about her work of art. On a relentless pursuit to learn everything she could about writing her first self-help book, we crossed paths. After listening to her story, there was no doubt in my mind that she was an "Extreme Winner". In her book, 'Running for My Life, The Diary of Alexis Love', Alexis turns a story of tragedy into one of triumph. A story that started out with pain and turned into one filled with purpose. While overcoming adversity and the cards life dealt her, she figured out the antidote to conquer almost anything life throws your way.

There could not have been a better author for this book. It takes a great deal of effort and dedication to commit to work that takes a lot of time and endurance. Alexis shows how pain, passion, and purpose has led her to live a life of perseverance. At 26 years old, Alexis is a Team USA athlete, two-time Olympic trial qualifier, motivational speaker, and resiliency analyst. I am sure Alexis's book will change the lives of millions. She shares what it takes to tap into your gift, discover your hidden talent, and find your inner strength.

This is one book you need to read because Alexis not only writes these words with passion, but she also lives a life filled with passion. Alexis knows that if she can rewrite her story, you can, too.

Pat Williams
Orlando Magic co-founder and senior vice president
Author of CHARACTER CARVED IN STONE

PROLOGUE

I have always wanted to tell this remarkable story about how I, Alexis Love, made it out of the storm! A story that most people would call a true testament of faith and resiliency. They say I am a strong individual but being strong comes easily to me. Strength, at one point, is all I had. Having strength is better than the word itself because when I think of the word strength, it reminds me that it comes with some type of action. It reminds me of the fighter I am at heart. And finally, strength is what you find deep inside when you are broken internally but still manage to smile on the outside. I was once told that to get past the most entangled and agonizing situations; the best approach is to face it head-on. You must stand up, fight, and be strong. If this is true, then why do we run from our past and the obstacles that have been put before us? Furthermore, why do we retreat from the struggles of everyday life if they are here to help us grow? What if these shortcomings were never meant to harm us? What if someone told you, the very thing you were running from in your early childhood, would be the one thing that would allow you to have the life you have always dreamed of? A life to love.

We all experience hardships at some point in our lives. When I was younger, I thought my adolescent years were the worst times ever; I hated my life because I had turned into the person I never wanted to be. I was depressed, unhappy, and filled with anger. Looking back, I pose this question to myself: What has changed? As I sat there and journaled in my diary, I stumbled upon the answer I was looking for. This usually happens when I write for a long time. I know everyone has their own perspectives about life, but for me, the answer was simple and clear. I began to change my mindset. I'm sure this new way of thinking was influenced by the books I have come across. Norman Vincent Peale said it best, "Change your thoughts, and you can change your world." I used to say I was running from my life but when asked, what is it about life that I am running from, I could not give a straight answer. However, I was certain about wanting to escape from my past. Crammed with pain and anger, I was running from the old me, but was afraid to embrace the new me. I was running in circles, until, one day, I had nowhere to run. That is when I realized, you can run in circles your whole life but there will come a time when you will be forced to decide self-destruction or trying something different. We all know that trying something different is not always the easiest thing to do, but I decided to take a leap of faith. Life taught me that you are only a prisoner to the cage you have allowed yourself to be trapped in.

I was not your typical middle school girl. I did not have a dream, in fact, I was living a nightmare and wanted to get away. I ran until I could not run anymore. I never stopped running. Track and Field became my escape; it saved my life. It was my safe-haven, the one place where I could feel completely liberated. Unlike other areas in my life, I had total control on the track, and no one could take that away from me. Eventually, that safe-haven helped me to realize that God had a plan for me this whole time.

I believe we all have a special gift or talent. Some of us know

Regardless of how many gifts we possess, each of us has something to give back to the world. The world needs your talent; the world needs you. I want to encourage you to tap into that gift, discover your hidden talent, and find your inner strength. I want you to know that you are more than a conqueror in Christ. I am sharing my life's story with the hope that you too will face those things which are keeping you from reaching your full potential. Your past does not define your future, but it will give you a concrete foundation. It is a story that you, and only you, can tell.

For a long time, I thought I was writing to myself in this "stupid diary," but I was writing to someone who could change everything in my life. To some, that may be an imaginary person, but to me, I look to God. From a dollar store diary with a key, to a grade school competition notebook, I have kept my story locked away, so I could share it with you. As you read my personal journal entries and look inside my inner thoughts, envision yourself living the life you will someday love. If I can do it, a girl who once hated everything about her life, you most certainly can too!

This diary will equip you with the power to conquer fear, hopelessness, doubt, and whatever else life throws your way. These pages are filled with my personal experiences to show you how I became victorious throughout the years. My purpose is to motivate and inspire families around the world, especially young women and teenagers.

Part I: Recognizing the Giant

The Intro to Alexis Love

The fact that someone knew me before I was formed in my mother's womb is beyond a mystery to me. Their sole purpose is having a plan for me to prosper in a world where so many fail. How could I not be anything but grateful? I am alive to tell my story, and that is one of God's greatest blessings to me. I am the youngest of four children. I was born on April 24th, 1991, to Jacqueline Anderson and Anthony Love Sr. in the beautiful city of Palmetto, Florida. With a population of about thirteen thousand people, Palmetto is in Manatee County, where some of the greatest athletes known to man were birthed. Curtis Johnson (Olympics), Tonja McKinney (Olympics), Anthony Love Jr (NFL), Dominique

Rodgers-Cromartie (NFL Cornerback) and Fabian Washington (Former NFL Cornerback), just to name a few. It is the one place where you can eat seafood almost every weekend and not be judged by any means. I say that with sarcasm as I sit here and reminisce about Grandma's huge pot of boiled seafood that she made with every peppered seasoning you can think of. You could smell the spicy aroma before you walk through the door. She used to cook those big jumbo crabs, the kind you could only get fresh from the back of a local fisherman's truck. Then she would whip up her old-fashioned homemade garlic butter sauce to smother them in. You would think Grandma Dora was about to start her own food truck! Well, at least that is what I had in mind every time I ran to the kitchen to fix my plate. That was how my weekends were spent as a child, and because my mother and grandmother were both from South Canton, Mississippi, one of their greatest assets was cooking soul food. It was not only a weekend tradition but a family tradition. Every Thanksgiving, Christmas, and birthday was spent gathered at one house to fellowship together, i.e., eat grandma's cooking. Until this day, I have not met another woman that can bake a Sweet Potato pie or a Red Velvet cake like she can.

My family did not live in a mansion, but we made the best out of what we had. Making the best with what I am given is me in a nutshell. I do not need a big fancy house and flashy things to be happy. When I was younger, I did not need them either. I just needed love. In fact, the times where I felt like I did not have much were the times I was the happiest. There were a lot of things that made me happy during those times.

From riding my bicycle with neighborhood friends to having street races with no shoes on. I enjoyed the times during the winter when my sisters and I put on more clothes than needed just so we could roll around in the grass and then later turn on our boom box to rehearse Destiny's Child's latest song. I find it funny that I always wanted to be Beyoncé but ended up being the tomboy out of my sisters. I could go on and on about the memories I had as a child. Another fond memory was racing to the kitchen when grandma yelled, "who wants to lick the spoon?!" Grandma always made her cakes from scratch, and you were lucky if you made it to the kitchen first to lick the icing off the spoon. Christmas time was some of the best times growing up because everyone got a chance to decorate the inside and outside of grandma's house. Oh, how I wish to be at that moment again. During those times of having little, no one required anything of me. I was living, breathing, and surviving. By surviving I mean having a roof over my head, food on the table, and clothes on my back. Trying to make something out of nothing was my mission because, at the time, you were considered fortunate if you had any hope of having a future. I was young, but I had seen and heard a lot, so accomplishing this mission of being a household name would mean the world to me, the future Alexis.

The greatest gift I gave myself at the age of nine years old was a diary. I saved my allowance for the week just so I could buy that diary. The diary was my getaway, my hiding spot where my mind could be completely free, and I would feel refreshed. It is where I kept my dream and goals written down. I never shared my dreams with anyone because I knew they were bigger than what others had expected of me.

I kept them all to myself. Besides, they were my dreams, my life and my diary. I was the only one who kept a key to that old, pink, raggedy diary. I took that thing everywhere with me. Without further delay, let us dive in.

Little Alexis

I was young, but I had a secret. It was more than a secret. It was a burden, one that I was never meant to carry on my own. The burden was so intense that I was sure I had developed quite a bit of anger that would turn into hate. It was the one thing every parent dread, and every child prays they never have to face. I experienced a form of childhood abuse. I thought growing up was supposed to be the best time of everyone's life. As I sat on the front porch, crying my eyes out, I realized that maybe I was wrong about that too. I did not know it at the time, but I was already beginning to grasp the concept: no one is exempt from pain, not even me. My age does not exempt me, love does not exempt me, and life is something I cannot escape from.

Daddy's Girl

I called my Dad, but I never told him my true feelings at the time. After talking to him, I felt much better, which is usually what happens after we talk for hours. Often, my dad is the only one that can get through to me. He reminded me that I have a roof over my head, I have clothes on my back and I have a dad that loves me. This was surely enough to be happy about, especially at my age. I used to sit at home and create this imaginary world where just my dad and I would take random trips around the world and enjoy life with no worries. I guess that came from my desire to want him to be happy because he always made me feel better, even in my darkest times. Besides the fact that he has never told me no, he is patient with me and never raises his voice. He is the one that always means business but knows how to get his point across without disrespecting the next person. He is not your typical army guy, but I like his demeanor. He is strongminded, kind, caring, and loving but still serious and straightforward when it comes to something he is passionate about.

I will never forget, I was in elementary school and my teacher asked if we had a hero, who it would be. With no surprise, I chose my dad as my hero. Of course, this turned into an assignment that was to be at least one paragraph long, so I wrote two. I had a lot to say about my hero. To others, he may seem like an ordinary person with a kind heart, but to me, he was far more than ordinary. He was more like a famous superhero in my eyes. I never saw him doing any wrong, but always lending a helping hand in the community and being the best firefighter, I know. He is very brave and caring. For example, I knew his job was serious, but it is even more risk-taking when you put your life on the line for others, talk about being selfless. He used to share stories about how he had to climb on enormous ladders to rescue people from tall burning buildings. He is so brave.

On Saturday afternoons, he would pick me up in his big pickup truck, so we could walk the Green Bridge together. The Green Bridge is a place in Bradenton, FL where people would go to walk and exercise. When he would call and say he was on his way, I would run to my room, pack an overnight bag, and wait by the front door. Weekends with my daddy were the best. If you have not figured it out by now, I am a daddy's girl. After waiting by the door and looking out of the kitchen window, if I caught the slightest glimpse of his big pick-up truck, I would sprint to the front door. He always made sure I gave him a hug before we started our adventures. He opened the door to the truck and would tell me that these are the things that boys are supposed to do. I never wanted those days to end. Slowly but surely, I was learning that there are some good people in this world and my dad showed me that. When I was down, my dad encouraged me. When I was sad, he showed me just how much he loved me. I truly think he was sent from the Guy above. My dad bought my first pair of track spikes and showed me at a very young age how a girl is supposed to be treated by opening the car door for me. I used to love our daddy-daughter dates. He was the first to introduce me to what I deserved and what to expect whenever I was old enough to date. Often, I wonder how he could teach me so much in such a short period of time on our weekend trips. Many times, I would hear others say, "You're just like your dad." They made that comment because I knew how to save my money, and I knew how to conduct business and be serious. I am proud to be just like my dad; obviously, I think highly of him.

Moving Away

I woke up one day and realized I was not sleeping beside my mama anymore and had not been for a while. I was in a new environment, and this time I had my own bed. There was a set of two bunk beds made from wood. I chose the top bunk, so I could hide my diary where no one would find it. Still in the same city but everything felt so new and unfamiliar. People came in and out periodically to check on us and do reports. I do not know who they were, but I know they meant business. All I know is that they came in with suits on and asked us, my brother and sisters, a ton of questions. I never knew what it meant, but I answered them and went back to my room to play with my Barbie dolls. Although I was too young to understand what was going on, that was my first encounter with a social worker. I was around the age of nine or so from what I can remember.

I may have been younger. Eventually I put the puzzle pieces together and concluded that I was now living with grandma because something did not go right at my mom's house.

I always had this thing where I try to play police and figure things out which could have been a good and bad thing for my age. I did not know how it would affect me later in life, but like everything else, it did. If I had known what an outer body experience was like, I am sure that would have been it. I am referring to the encounter with a social worker, not that it was weird, but often it left me confused. There were times when I found myself daydreaming and wishing things were different. Even if things were different regarding my living situation, I was too young to know what was best for me, so I just rolled with it. Even so, that upbringing taught me a lot about life. To highlight a few things, my grandmother taught me how to cook, clean, and do laundry with the towels folded just right to fit in the linen closet. I will never forget the times we were told to be home before the street lights came on, now that was a real race to the front door. Although we never found out what would happen if we weren't, I sure as heck did not want to know. From driving us to the kid's choir rehearsal at church to making sure my sisters and I were up early Saturday mornings to cheer for the Rubonia Rattlers, somehow grandma made it work. So overall the move may have been the best thing at that time for my siblings and me.

I did what most kids did in their early childhood. I loved watching Disney movies and pretending like I was baking with my Easy Bake Oven. Movies like the Lion King, Little Mermaid, and Matilda are my favorite movies of all time.

After watching the Lion King, I felt like I could conquer the world and be the next big thing. It reminded me of who I was and what I could accomplish when I got older. The Little Mermaid took my imagination to another level, I began to think of doing the impossible, I started to think of supernatural things. And of course, Matilda, everyone loved Matilda, and I am sure I am not the only one who has tried to get mad enough to make the door slam shut or make the refrigerator open by using a secret power. These are the things that made me feel like I belonged, even though when I was not staying with my mother. Let me tell you about her.

Mama's Baby

Jack Rabbit is what they call her! She is fly, flashy and full of joy! One thing I can say, she knows how to entertain a crowd. You could tell when she got a good kick out of something because her one gold tooth in the front would show after a good laugh. I love everything about her, even when she seems to talk loud with that Mississippi accent of hers. My mother and I have this unbreakable bond. By the time I was in middle school and ready to hear some real-life stories, she shared her personal experience about being at the abortion clinic. The story goes like this, she walked into the abortion clinic and as she was on the operating table, the doctor did an ultrasound and came back with unexpected news. He looks up at my mom and says, "It has a heartbeat." My mom stretched her eyes wide open with a surprising look on her face. The doctor asked if she would like to proceed. My mom looks up, she said boldly,

"Unhook me and get me off of this table." She said there is

no way she could abort a child knowing that it had a heartbeat. She took the four hundred dollars that was for the abortion and went Christmas shopping for my sisters and brother. I am sure you have figured it out by now, that baby in her stomach was me! 'Til this day, she calls me her miracle baby. Before I was out of my mother's womb, I faced adversity and I beat it. My mom constantly reminds me that I am special, and I am not here by accident. Thank you, Mama. I love you more than you will ever know.

Monsters Are Real

I have never been fond of scary movies. I would not watch a horror film if it was dark outside or past 8pm. By the way, whoever made the statement, "Monsters are not real" just flat out lied. There are real-life monsters here on earth. Some are in the streets, some are in the schools, some are at the playground, and some may be in our homes. Maybe it is another illusion or another one of my crazy thoughts because I tend to have those more often these days. Who was I fooling, this was real, and the things I experienced were real. But just like the cartoons and scary movies, we dare not to watch after sunset, if we do not speak of them then maybe they will go away, or we can force it to the back of our minds. That way it is not real. I was afraid of the dark for a long time, but then I realized the dark was where I could sit just to get away from the world; I never really understood that. The one place I was afraid of was the one place I ran to for my escape, but it would only make me more depressed. When I came out of the room, I felt the same way I did when I entered it. I was always expecting something different, something uplifting but it was false hope. I have always wondered what life would be like if someone, anyone, would have walked into my room to turn on the light. I only wanted one person, just one, to walk into my bedroom to ask if I needed to talk. That was typical for me, closed in my bedroom and sitting in the dark, waiting to be rescued. For me, it was deeper than the physical movement of a switch, it was the light I needed to ignite on the inside.

Maybe I should start getting on my knees every night to pray. I love God, and I know he will do great things for me, but sometimes when I am in deep thought, I question if God exists. I was under the assumption that if He is who all the adults say He is then these things would not be happening to me. Why can I not hide from the monster? He always finds me. I have sworn a million times that I would no longer have to write in my diary, but here I am again, writing until my fingers hurt from gripping the gel pen. One of my biggest fears is facing reality. I may not understand what is happening, but I do know this, it is wrong. I have experienced pain and hurt at an early age. One incident after the next made it that much harder for me to trust people, especially men.

Sometimes, I am too smart for my own good. The one thing I do know, however, is that I am a lost little girl, screaming on the inside but silent on the outside. What made me silent? It was fear. Fear of rejection, fear of no one listening to me, and fear of the truth. I was not ready to confront my condemning thoughts. One thing I am grateful for is Grandma Dora. She made sure we were dressed, fed, and in Sunday school and church every Sunday. Even with attending church faithfully, I still felt alone, abandoned, and dysfunctional. Monster or no monster, I was afraid of what I might see in the mirror. Would it be a nice reflection of me or someone I turned into that I was never intended to be? I was sure of this one thing, I needed a way out. A way to escape the reality of what was happening to me.

Looking for Love

After experiencing a form of child abuse, I was lost. I was confused and could not make simple distinctions between right and wrong. I often wondered why no one questioned my behavior in elementary school. I was placed in speech class and could not comprehend simple words and phrases. I had trouble interpreting short paragraphs and books. It was plain to see, my mind was clouded, and my vision was blurry. I felt as though I was looking at life through a large magnifying glass but still could not see the picture clearly. If anything, the picture was smaller because I could not see a way out.

When you are vulnerable at such a young age, it is so easy to be misguided. I felt misguided from the truth and set apart from the world. I was in my own league. I felt as if I was falling from a mountain of pain with no one to catch me. I was far away, to the point of no return. I never knew what love was, so I was looking for love in the all the wrong places. I was looking for love in things, especially material things I sure as heck could not buy for myself. Whatever I perceived to be love, I went with it. Some find love in words, some find love in actions, for me, it was the simple utterance of the four-letter word. I wanted someone to say it to me; it sounded good, just like everything else I had heard in the past. I thought that if a person says they love you, then they mean it. I wish I had known that not everyone is true to their words. After all, how could I recognize what I have never seen or felt? This is not a trick question; the answer was clear, it was impossible. I mean my friends lived in homes with both parents, but I was confused. I was not confused about my parents and the way they loved me, but I was confused about other incidents. The only thing I could look forward to was being alive. As I got older, I started to notice that everyone was involved in something whether it was a sport, dance group, or school play. Now that I am in middle school and my friends all seem to be too busy for me, I need to find something to do. To keep myself busy so I would not have to return home right after the end of a school day. I desperately wanted to be a part of something, anything. At least we had church events and outings that kept us busy, so I am not complaining.

Intro to Sports

Don't get me wrong, I enjoyed going to Sunday School and hearing the elders sing those old hymns before we were called to the front of the altar to answer questions. I still remember we would read over small white flash cards and have a quiz at the end. The cards taught us basic principles and information about the bible. We would memorize a verse or two, then walk into the sanctuary for the overall review. I remember those times because Sunday school at Shining Light C.O.G.I.C is where I met one of my best friends, Yasmine Waiters. She was so polite. She was one of those girls that everyone admired growing up because of her long healthy hair and cute manicured nails. She was someone I looked up to even though she was only a year and one week older than me. We would always joke about that because both our birthdays were in April. One day, Yasmine invited me to a track practice. I was twelve years old, innocent, and shy as ever. I did not know what sports all were about, but I knew how to be disciplined because I learned that living with my grandmother. I thought to myself, "Hey, why not?" If I can wake up every Saturday morning to do my chores, then surely, I can try out for track and field. I can only fail if I do not try, right? Well, at least that is what everyone else says. I was so embarrassed because of the simple reason that I was going to try out for a new sport, but I did not have a sports bra or running shoes. Despite not having what I needed, Yasmine was nice enough to share her sports bras with me. I mean we were only twelve and thirteen, so we wore the same bra size.

So, we arrive at what is now my first day of track practice. I did not know what to expect, but I did not want to be left home alone after school, so track practice was the next best thing. It is not that I was reconsidering my decision to go to track practice, I just did not know what to expect. I have always wanted to be a part of a team, but I was so afraid to try something new. As I ran my first warm-up lap, I started to build up confidence and get this feeling of peace I had never felt before. With each step, left foot then right, I felt a sense of security for the first time in my life. I felt as though I had total control, and nothing could stop me. I was beginning to learn something new about me, and I was open to whatever it was the universe was trying to teach me through track. It was a joy I could not explain! I made the track team, and it meant the world to me. It gave me a feeling I cannot put into words. It was amazing! I was finally getting something right after thinking I was at fault for everything that happened in my early childhood years. I survived the first day of practice. I made it, I was officially part of the Manatee Mustangs AAU Track and Field Team in Bradenton, FL. Track was big in states like Florida and Texas. People would joke and say, "It must be something in the water because Florida breeds fast athletes." I would laugh and say, "If only they knew what our real motivation was."

I cannot speak for every athlete, but upon my research, I do know that most athletes were birthed from a struggle, depending on the circumstance. I also found that some people, including myself, are lost in search of their "identity," which seems to be a universal matter. Everyone has their special gifts and talents, but mine happens to be track and field at this point. I would love to say that my path to success was easy, but that is far from the truth. Being raised in a small town where many people want success but very few obtain it was a challenge.

To be honest, I had a different mindset by the age of twelve. I can recall sitting in detention hall, thinking to myself, what if I started paying attention in class and being a good student? What if I joined the local AAU track team and was great at it, or what if I could attend college and make a name for myself? For me, that is what it took, a change in my thought process and self-motivation like no other. I knew a change was needed for me to make it out. But I was faced with this question: How do I make it out? Meaning, what will it take for me to be a product of my environment in a good way and not fall victim to poverty. This question was poised way before I knew poverty was one's mindset. That is how I began this journey of becoming the new me.

Being content with where you are will eventually lead to mediocracy. Something I do not want. Okay, I cannot go any further without sharing my experience about my very first track meet. I was twelve years young, and I was so nervous that I forgot to tie my shoelaces. My dad ordered my new track spikes, but it took a while for them to be mailed out, so I ran in some all-white Nike shoes that had no grip on the bottom. They were not running shoes, just some regular ol' white tennis shoes, but I did not care. I knew I was ready to put my skills to the test, nervous but ready. Before I walked out on the track, Coach Tonya McKinney told me to recite Philippians 4:13, "I can do all things through Christ." She said if at any time, I was scared, to think of this verse and I would feel better. I followed her instructions. I warmed up and stretched with the team, walked over to the big white check-in tent, and waited for my heat to start. The heat is the group of other girls you will be called out on the track with to run against. Typically, there are eight-nine lanes on the track. Moving on to the next phase, the officials were all there with their blue and red striped shirts, dressed in a straw hat, ready to start the race. The official's hat was a key element here in Florida because it is always so hot. I ran the 200-meter dash from start to finish, I knew nothing or no one would be able to stop me. I won that race! Nervous, one shoe on halfway through the race, and in my regular ol' Nikes. If you were wondering, it was an amateur move, I forgot to double-knot my shoelaces so the more I ran, the looser my shoe got until it eventually went flying off. I knew then and there if I could win a race with one shoe on, who knows how far I could go with this track thing. I obviously ran with one shoe on because of my level of nervousness before starting the race, but I was ready! Rule number one; always double knot your shoes before running a race. Now I was excited and looking forward to a future in track.

Word spread around town that there was an up and coming female athlete in Palmetto, FL. I was getting invites to workout with personal trainers on the weekend and other perks. Not knowing the trainers worked with mostly football players, I took the offers. At this point, if it involved running, I was going to be there. Before I was a part of the AAU Team, I knew I was fast from the time I raced boys that were much older than me on the old baseball field at The Rubonia Community Center. This center is where my siblings and I went to summer camp after school was out. It was a place that had everything you needed. This was where I learned the true meaning of, "it takes a village to raise a child." The staff that took care of us while attending the community center made a huge impact on my life, some I will never forget. Whether it was supervising us on field trips, arts, and crafts or teaching us about being a pre-teen and mannerism. Sometimes that is all a kid ever wants in life, someone that cares and listens to them; well at least that is what I wanted. At the community center, I met friends who were also into sports. This was the start of me being a track fan. I loved running!

The early mornings on the grass fields at Lincoln Park paid off. I used to think I was crazy or this extreme tomboy for working out with football players on Saturday mornings and being the only female out there, but I can say the ladder drills and hills worked for me. I did not have a lot of confidence the first day I started running but doing the extra work on the weekends gave me the boost I needed for high school track. I was not afraid; I was ready for something new. Not knowing what to expect, I was embracing it all. Soon it was time to move on to high school sports and what it had to offer. I wanted to run with the big girls.

High School Track

Before I could finish my full week as a freshman at Palmetto High School, the track coaches had already introduced themselves. Coach Robert Kelly and Coach Roderick Martin are two I will never forget. The two of them were like peanut butter and jelly; you could not have one without the other. They were similar in their approach to coaching because of their passion for the sport but also understanding enough to know what I needed as an individual. I met Coach Martin while eating lunch under the red covered patio area. If I do not remember anything else, I remember these words, "Alexis, you have a God-given talent, and you will do amazing things on the track." I will never forget what he said. Besides my dad's words of encouragement, I heard another human being believes in me. I can tell that he was a man of his word. From that point on, I looked up to Coach Martin. He was also a math teacher, so when he had a quick break, I would get the bathroom pass to visit his class just to hear a word of encouragement. He told me to know my self-worth and that I am too pretty to be worrying about the knucklehead boys here on campus. That was all new to me. I had always thought I was messed up in the head and that I was a mistake. Not sure why I had those feelings, but I am almost positive it had something to do with being picked on as a child. It was so ironic because soon after I had this conversation with Coach Martin, I found myself falling in love with Jasmon. He did not like his name, so everyone called him Chico. We had so much in common! Our upbringing was very similar. I was convinced, we were meant to be, and Chico was going to be my husband someday. I know, I know, it could have been puppy love, but it felt real. He did something that no other boy had done at my high school. He respected me. Not for my looks or anything else but he respected me as a young lady. He only wanted to be my best friend and love me. Chico was known for his artistic abilities; boy was he talented. You could literally tell him your life story and he could draw a picture of it. One word: Amazing! I could not get enough of him. I do not know what was better, staying on AOL Instant Messenger until 3am or sneaking out of class to meet in the hallways for a quick hug. Chico and I were picture perfect. I looked forward to seeing his face every day.

I was shy my first track season, but who would not be. I was a freshman running on the junior team, and when that ended, I was running Varsity. Running on the varsity track team as a freshman was cool. My first year on the track consisted of learning the program and getting familiar with having teammates to push me. All in all, it was a good situation for me and a good start to my high school track career. Although I was always nervous and found myself concerned with the upperclassman at other schools, it turned out okay. Somehow, the nervousness and adrenaline gave me the energy I needed to run down the track full speed. AAU Track was fun but my freshman year at Palmetto High was the real deal. I started to learn the importance of working together as a team. Whether it was cheering for others from the sidelines or counting aloud while we were stretching, I learned a sense of accountability. There were individual events, but now I will be responsible for moving the baton around the track with three other girls. As nervous as I was in ninth grade, I managed to do much better than I expected. Before the school year was over, Coach Kelly and Coach Martin both promised me a spot on the varsity team if I continued to work hard and not quit. That gave me a bit of confidence going into my sophomore year.

I was ready to see what sophomore year had to offer. Besides being boy crazy and trying to get popular by doing all the wrong things, I have learned a lot. I have learned that I am too young to really understand love, but I am also old enough to know that giving up my treasure for temporary pleasure is only putting me out there in a bad light. Great! I am building my reputation, but it is not good at all. I do not think I am all that pretty with my big forehead and big lips, but the boys seem to like it; at least that is what they tell me. I think Chico was the only one who meant what he said when he told me I was beautiful. Somehow, I manage to sabotage our relationship by not being completely faithful. Everything was fine until I fed into the lies people planted inside my head. Me being me, having trust issues, I did what I thought was best; moved on. Of course, that did not last long because I would see his face and fall in love all over again. So back and forth we went. One day in a relationship with his pictures on my Myspace page to I am not sure again. I wish I was not so bad with decision making. I hate my life at times, but I love myself for the unique person I am because I know there will never be another me and that is what makes me unique. I love myself because I know that no one else can walk in my shoes and be strong enough to deal with the cards life has dealt me.

like I was cursed or something. During these times, I had bad relationship break-ups, some my fault and others were not; I was over it. I cheated on my boyfriends, they cheated on me, and it was a big mess. So, I came up with this idea, since the guys hurt me, why not see how many I can meet and hurt in the process. After my freshman year, I was convinced that they are all after one thing. The one thing my brother Courtney warned me about. I guess it is easy to say what you will not do until you are faced with the situation. I am looking forward to a new year, new beginnings, new chances, and a new way to deal with life's problems. I just need to improve on things like having more self-respect and increasing my self-esteem. I just prayed things would get better.

In the summer, my family always took a vacation to Canton, Mississippi to visit my mom's side of the family. Most of the time we traveled around the fourth of July. We drove a full thirteen hours; luggage packed tight, sometimes on the roof of the van depending on the trunk space. Uncle Dave would be the lead driver. He was so familiar with the routes that he knew all the shortcuts and back roads. Uncle Dave was that one uncle that gave you money for every birthday. For example, if you were turning fifteen, you would get fifteen dollars from Uncle Dave and sometimes a little extra if you stood there a little longer with a smile on your face. He always calls me his beautiful niece. Come to think of it, I am not sure if I have ever seen Uncle Dave upset, he always kept a smile on his face. Now we are a couple hours into the drive, and everyone is sound asleep, but grandma Dora makes the announcement, with her loud Mississippi accent, "Okay y'all get up, we are about to ride through the tunnel." That was our thing, waking up to pass through the tunnel in Mobile, Alabama. It was like a tradition for us, or maybe to me it was the illusion of going through a closed in space at a super-fast pace.

Since my introduction to running, I was infatuated with fast things. After taking random breaks for food and gas, we finally made it to Canton, Mississippi and the family was waiting outside anticipating our arrival. They met us at Aunt Reeda's house. Not that the house was very big, but it was full of love, and I would rather stay there than a hotel any day. Waking up to Aunt Reeda's smoked red sausage and cheese grits was the highlight of my day. We got there on a Thursday, but Friday is when things really got off to a good start. A good ol' fish fry and some fried chicken was the choice of meal on family day. So, we stayed on vacation for a short period usually two weeks and then we ended the visit on the weekend of the Fourth of July. For some reason, it always seemed to be on the weekend for us. I could never tell because time seems to go by so fast when you are having fun. Mississippi was always fun because you have that one auntie that never stops dancing and that one uncle that will not put the beer down. It was all fun and games still. I could not wait to put on my new red, white and blue outfit. I loved the feeling of having fresh clothes and some new shoes. It made me feel like a new person. After lighting fireworks and stuffing my face, it is time to return to the Sunshine State; Florida to get ready for another school year.

Lord, if I would have known losing IT meant possibly losing You; then I would have waited. When I have a daughter, I will tell her that losing her virginity is not a way to earn popularity or get attention. It is, in fact, her golden treasure. A lock, in which she holds the key.

Just Wait

She used to give it away, so they could have their way... with her. Not knowing that it was a secret treasure she could never get back. It was the key to a lock that should have never been opened. Is it wrong to do the wrong thing if you do not know what the right thing is? Or is she wrong for chasing something that she would later regret in her adult years? It is almost like a curse, a temptation that will not leave her alone. Or is it the small voice telling her that it is ok to do wrong. Her body is a temple, and she knows it is not hers. I wonder if she will ever know the true meaning of a woman's self-worth. The value, the beauty of being loved first. But broken is what she remains, and they tell her love hurts. It is an addiction, an attraction, all the above but how can you say no to the one you love. It is easy, trust your gut and stay in the word. Instead of feeling guilty as the world turns. I guess the moral of the story is that we all need somebody but not their body.

Just wait. Set the date.

1 Corinthians 6:19 "Do you not know that your bodies are temples of the Holy Spirit, who is in you, whom you have received from God. You are not your own;

It is here, sophomore year of my high school career. It almost seems like my freshman year just ended yesterday. Maybe this year will be different. Even though I am in Intensive Reading and Intensive Math, my schedule is cool so far. No real complaints about my other classes at all and my teachers seem to care about me. Now we are not even a month in, and I feel depressed about something that took place over the summer. Nothing that I am proud of, to say the least. God, I just want people to look at me differently. Why did I feed into the lies? Feed into the void. At times, I wish this whole thing was a dream. I wish I was invisible but wishes are just hopes for something that is not easily attainable. I feel as if most of my problems stem from my childhood. I always wondered how things would have been if I would have had a better childhood growing up. Please understand this, I was well taken care of, but I am speaking in terms having someone be emotionally there for me to talk to. I know I am only in high school, but when I get older, I promise to never mistreat my kids. I am not sure if certain people in my family are too blind to see what is going on in my life or if they choose not to see, but I think I am going to journal and set my boundaries and rules for myself. This is what I came up with so far:

1) Do not go below my expectations.

2) Ignore boys and their rude comments.

3) Have self-confidence and smile more.

That should be a good start for me. God, no one understands me. Why could I not be the perfect child in the family? I do not know if I am wrong for thinking that things were my fault or maybe I had never heard that they were not. It was easy for me to want to be the perfect child because it seems like perfect people do not have "messed up" lives and they seem happier. Maybe I need a real friend, someone that I could talk to and share my secrets with. To be honest, I am not sure if that will ever happen. The girls that I thought were my friends are always talking behind my back, and maybe they have a reason to. I cannot seem to figure out why I continue to make poor choices when it comes to boys. It did not really affect my way of thinking until the beginning of my sophomore year. It got worse and worse. The thoughts that were going through my head and what I was telling myself.

These words keep playing over and over in my head like an old CD that has been scratched a million times, "TRUST ME." I really believed him, but this time I think I learned my lesson. It is funny how you can meet someone; fall in love, but then when something goes wrong, it is like you never met that person. I guess this was the "puppy love" or "fake love" my brothers Courtney and AJ warned me about. I found myself in the very situation I said I was going to avoid this school year. I am starting to think that life is a messed-up test that you must live through to see if you can make it. If you ask me, I have already failed. I am really trying my best to make it and not to run away. I am getting to that point where I cannot find one minute out of the day when I am happy. I realize that regretting what I did will not change anything. I need a real counselor, a psychologist or something. I am not even sure if a counselor would help at this point. I do know one thing; I am way too young to have self-defeating or suicided thoughts. Either that or I will soon plan my runaway.

There is only so much I can tell my guidance counselor at school, Ms. Moyer. For some reason, I feel as though she already knows what I am going through before I say a word. I go sit in her office just to have a piece of candy and watch her do paperwork. I am usually fine until she would ask me the questions that no one seems to ask, "My dear, how are you?" That is when the tears would fall like a river that never ends. Without saying much, she would walk around her desk to embrace me. Most of the time that is all I needed, a hug and for someone to tell me that everything would be okay. I get home and isolate myself, back into a corner and write in my journal. Because I am a little older now, I will not call it my diary anymore; I will call it my secret journal. I keep telling myself that if I can just get over my horrible past, then everything would be okay. It sounds easy, but it is the one thing that is holding me back. I feel it; I feel the weight of a heavy burden pulling me down. Strange thing though, I do not want the person who betrayed me as a little girl to go to jail because that defeats the purpose. Vengeance does not belong to me.

Now I am more concerned with the rumors at school. I always say I could care less about what other people are saying, but the truth is I do care. I am so tired of being alone and trapped, feeling like I have no one to talk to. I just hope that someday this pain I feel inside will serve its purpose in my life.

On the track side, everything is good, but I am having trouble breathing in the middle of practice so the ladies at the school clinic said I should get that checked out as soon as possible. My appointment is with a cardiologist in Tampa, FL. He is presumed to be one of the best. After a full day of tests, including a stress test, the doctor said it was not from stress which was surprising, but he diagnosed me with exercise-induced asthma. Perfect way of saying, I am taking a risk daily by running track, so it is my call if I decide to quit running, but I cannot. It is the one thing that has been constant in my life since the age of twelve. I am fifteen now. I cannot give up or have someone try to take that away from me. I have a relationship with track now. Sometimes it is good, and other times it is bad, but I am willing to stick with it to the end. Track is somewhat of a parent to me; it teaches me those things I was looking for as a little girl. It taught me to never give up, it taught me how to be tough, it taught me how to believe in myself and at this point, it is the one place I feel secure. When I am down in the starting blocks, I am at peace. I feel unstoppable at the start line. When the gun goes off, I can no longer see or hear anything, it is just me and the track. The world is at a standstill, and I feel as though I can conquer the world. It is my safe-haven, my escape.

To summarize the doctor's visit, he said he would not sign my release to run; which I understood because if anything happened to me on the track, he would be responsible. This was my introduction to faith. I never understood the word, but I was acting on it before I knew it. Of course, we attended Sunday school and church, but I did not understand this God thing. In fact, I am not even sure if He is real because if he were, then I would not be having these crazy thoughts of harming myself, even years later. I am not sure if I know who God is. I could not believe it. Did I just write that? I was attending church, Sunday School and Wednesday night bible study before I can remember and here I am, in high school still questioning my beliefs. I walk around asking people to pray for me, and I am not praying for myself. I just want everyone to know the real Alexis Love. In the middle of the school year, the school held assemblies about self-esteem issues and bullying. I liked to believe they helped me but to others, you can see that it was a way for them to skip their last class of the day. At the end of the program, we made a declaration out loud, in front of everyone. It started like this, "I am Alexis, and if you knew me, you would know that I like to dance, listen to music, polish my nails, and hang out with my friends, etc." I like the idea of changing someone's perspective of you because it is so easy to judge. It is in us to judge others before we take the time to know them.

I wonder what life would be like if we had these intervention programs earlier, teaching us that everyone is different and being different is not a bad thing. For some reason, I always forget to mention track when I am meeting new people. I do not know if I assume they know or if I am afraid to share something that is so dear to my heart. After all, I felt like I did not deserve anything that was good. If I won a race, I would think it was by pure luck. Not because I worked hard and sweated in practice but maybe my opponents were tired that day, and they let me win. My accomplishments did not feel like accomplishments, it felt like I was in search to satisfy someone or something, never doing it for myself. For example, my sophomore year, the nervousness was a lot better than my freshman year, but something was still missing. I did not believe in myself. In fact, the better I got on the track, the harder I was on myself. I was operating from a place of depression.

Often, I would feel as though the world would be a better place without me. Despite all the negative thoughts I had daily, I knew that one thing could change everything; track. Track and Field is my focus and I know one day it will make me money. Sometimes I wonder like dang, is this track thing really what I want to do. I want to prove to others that I can and will be somebody. I will run to the best of my ability. So, I guess yes is the answer for track. I cannot believe for a split-second I was thinking about giving it up. Outside of track, I feel like I am throwing my life away. I get so emotional after track season. I feel so bad right now. Maybe I was not meant to be here. Dear God, nobody understands me. I mean why does it always have to be me with the problems? Why, why, why, why, why, why? Aside from everything else, I do believe there is a Heaven and hell, and hell is not a place I am trying to go.

She was hurt and abused at a young age. Somehow, they still seem to think she had it made. I am amazed at the way she turned out. They said she would be pregnant at a young age, without a doubt. They said she wouldn't make any money running track. One day she left town and said she was never coming back. She used to run from the pain then it finally caught her. She never thought she would smile again. Then she saw her face on CNN. Trying to escape the pain inside but could not hold it in. They say she has pretty eyes but never asked how many tears she has cried. And on top of that, she still managed to rise. The world is coming to an end and this she already knows. And the only thing she wants to do is try to live Holy. She made it through the struggle. She made it through the pain but heartbroken is what she remains.

It is now my junior year of high school. This is the time when things started to unfold in my life. I was beginning to earn respect differently. I went from having people whisper behind my back during lunch to having people want to sit with me at lunch. They went from standing behind me to cheering me on and standing beside me. There is a difference between the two. Something was beginning to change on the inside; I let out a sigh of relief. Track and field has given me a way out, and I cannot stop smiling. Now Coach Martin and Coach Kelly are talking to me about national signing day, which will be held during my senior year. National Signing Day is huge! It is when all the high school athletes commit to the university or college of their choice and most of the time it is open to the public. They are pushing me to keep my grades and test scores above average and everything is working out. I do not have nearly as much girl drama as I had the first two years. I guess the old saying is true, "some things get better with time." Maybe my situation changed, maybe I changed, or just maybe the universe is on my side this time. I had a happy ending to my sophomore year on the track and running at the Regional and State Meet. This is a good feeling. By this time, I was working as an office aid during the second half of my class schedule, so everyone considered me a teacher's pet, but I cannot argue with that. I was only doing my job to get the best grade possible. Besides, the class was not difficult at all. Under Mrs. Ann and others in the office, I learned about time management, how to file paperwork, send faxes and other skills I would need in the real world. I enjoyed my junior year, but I was more excited about being a senior.

My senior year was everything and more! How exciting it was to think about prom, going to college, and having the best year on the track all at once. Not to sound arrogant, but I was running with the popular crowd now. Everyone wants to be associated with a winner and by this time, I had earned the name, Manatee County's Top Female Sprinter. I am not making this up. You can check the newspaper articles.

During my senior year, 2009, I was the only female athlete to travel alone to the Class 3A State Track Meet. I did it! I was one of the fastest female runners in the state of Florida. I had made a name for myself! My grades are good, I am focused, no more drama and the depression is slowly fading away. Chico and I decided to be close friends and stay in touch. Well, we stayed in touch but that ended up being another part of our love story. We were dating, again. My friends are supportive, and my dad is still standing in bleachers at every track meet. Life is great. Who knew, little Alexis Love would find her way out.

I remember back in 2009, the same Nike shoebox I used to do my science project on the great Machu Picchu, is the same shoebox I stuffed my college offer letters in. Coming home to a letter from a university was like coming home to a Christmas gift every day. It was so predictable, yet unexpected at the same time. It reminded me of the movie Blindside where Michael Oher had meetings with coaches in the living room, going through the motions but not fully understanding what was happening. I did not know much about college sports or recruiting, but I knew I wanted to attend college, and, if possible, run track. I had no idea could get a full-ride scholarship to attend a four-year university. Ms. Moyer, Coach Martin, and Coach Kelly all tried to explain this to me, but it was not registering.

It was the beginning of 2009, and it was time to take my first official track visit to one of the three schools I had my eyes on. My top three choices were The University of South Florida, The Florida State University, and Murray State University. I was familiar with the two in Florida because my siblings were attending school there, but Murray State University, located in Murray, Kentucky was unfamiliar territory. Everything was still new to me, I was learning as I was going. I remember having phone calls in the evenings from different coaches, and over time I eventually established who my favorites were. The Head Coach at Murray State said something the other universities had not mentioned in our previous conversation. Two words: full-ride. He explained that everything would be covered by one single scholarship. Included in that scholarship was my dorm room, meal plan, classes, and books. My responsibility was to show up, train hard, and perform when I was called. I was still sold on USF, but I decided to take a visit to Murray. I was always curious about what was outside of the state of Florida.

It was my first time being on an airplane, I was nervous and excited at the same time, but I was ready to take on a new adventure all by myself. Even my fear of heights did not stop me from this big opportunity. My dad pulled into my grandmother's driveway, on time as usual. He says it is good to be at the airport two hours early just in case anything goes wrong, but in his case, he was early to every occasion. I arrived at the airport, checked my bags, and went on to board the plane. It was weird because although I was afraid of flying, I preferred the window seat so that I could see the landing. From the time, I took my seat on the plane, all I could imagine was being a college student and doing something I know some of my family members had not done. I wanted to make my folks happy! I could barely keep my composure. The plane landed a little rough but that was expected, I guess. There is no airport in Murray, KY, so I flew into Nashville, TN which was nice. It was not too bad being that it was my first time flying and alone at that. The head Coach picked me up, and we drove almost two hours back to Murray. I listened to him explain the whole collegiate process as I stared out the window looking at mountains for the first time in my life. It was like the movies; the ones where everything seems so peaceful. For a moment, I felt like I had escaped life's problems and the happy ending was soon to come. I remember planning to attend the school simply because I would see mountains quite often. The coach mentioned the cold weather but never mentioned snow in our previous conversations. Besides the fact that it was snowing during our drive and I was told that it did not snow in Kentucky, I was looking forward to being a Murray State "Racer." That's the school mascot, well a thoroughbred if you want to be specific.

We arrived at the university, and I was immediately paired with a host that would show me around and pretty much tell me all there was to know about being a collegiate athlete. Her name was Amber, she was perfect. She was one of those girls on the team who had it all together, studied even on the weekends and did not get distracted. I knew she would be someone I could look up to for the years to come. I was excited because we could find the USF football game on TV while being in the dorm room. I was always excited to see my brother, AJ, play. He was my inspiration.

He was living out a dream, and I wanted to follow in his footsteps. I got this unexplainable feeling inside when I saw that big bold number five flash across the television screen. It screamed, "IT IS POSSIBLE," well at least for me. Amber answered all my questions and gave me a few extra pointers on how to prepare myself for college. Everything was smooth as far as the visit went. I met everyone in the athletic department, toured the campus, and then ended the night with a nice team dinner. It was one of the best experiences of my life! It was life-changing, to say the least. I could not wait to get back to Palmetto, FL to tell my family all about it. The visit alone was a huge deal because where I am from, we call that "making it out" and if you make it, then you are considered successful. The visit was short, but it was enough to convince me to verbally commit a few weeks later.

I arrived at the Tampa International airport, grabbed my suitcase, and walked out to see my dad's big truck waiting for me and ready to give me a loving hug. On the forty-five-minute drive home I told my dad all about the visit, how nice the girls on the track team were, and how the football stadium only had one side, but that it was a cool site to see.

Now it is time to get back to Palmetto High School and make some decisions, of course, it is not that easy, it never is. I came home to another voicemail from the University of South Florida. By this time, I am somewhat familiar with the whole official and unofficial visit thing, so I decided to take an unofficial visit to USF the following weekend. I asked my dad to drive me there because I thought it would be cool if we ran into my brother while touring the campus. For some odd reason, I always liked that school. So, there we were, my dad and I, on a peaceful sunny Saturday, exploring the university. I liked almost everything about that campus, including the underwater treadmills in the training room and the girls track locker room. It was everything I had dreamed of except for one thing, the amount the scholarship offered. While Murray State was offering a full-ride, USF at the time, was not. I had a decision to make. Do I attend the school that is close to home and try to work my way up to a full ride or do I move fourteen hours away to a state I have never lived in and make the most of it?

I am sure I ran Coach Martin and Coach Kelly crazy at the time. It was my senior year in high school so every chance I got while being an office aid, I would sit in their offices to talk. Then I would sneak away and go talk to my favorite guidance counselor, Ms. Moyer. I would walk into her office and without hesitation, she put her candy dish out front just for me. She listened to me talk for a while, gave me local scholarship applications, and after an hour or so she would say, "Okay Alexis my dear, I have to get back to work," I never wanted to leave her office, but I understood that she had work to do. She is one of the people who had a major impact on my life in high school. Always believing in me and telling me that I can achieve, not some of my goals, but all of them. I am extremely grateful to have had a caring school guidance counselor like her.

National Signing Day is quickly approaching, and they are getting the library set up for the big day. Although I was looking forward to this day, it was the most difficult decision I would have to make for my life. I did not know what to expect, I just knew I would have to roll with whatever decision I made. Now to the day every high school athlete looks forward to but is not certain about what to expect. National Signing Day! The one day you think you are signing your life away, but it is just a stepping stone to get you to the next level. The day I was excused from class to sit in the library/media room to show the world that I, Alexis Love, was not afraid of moving far away to accomplish a goal I set myself. By far away, I mean fourteen hours to be exact. Moving forward, I was confident. Track taught me more about myself than life ever could during my high school career. So, it is here, the cameras are set up, the school media is in place, and both local and national news stations are here. Myself and a few others athlete's I was friends with, were ready for our big day. I sat there with my black silk shirt on and my new grey slacks I had just bought from Beauls Outlet; I was ready to sign my life away, as they would say. My classmate, Damian Copeland, signed to the University of Louisville and my other classmate, Ked Johnson, signed to the University of Florida. Now the cameras are on me. I picked up the Murray State hat, and there you have it; Alexis Love will be attending Murray State University in the Fall of 2009!

Now it is time to finish the year out strong, keep my grades up, and take the ACT and SAT. You know, all the fun stuff to prepare for college. In the meantime, I am packing and getting things in order. At the same time while trying to keep my mind off leaving behind the love of my life. Ms. Debra, my brother and sister's mom, bought my first laptop. My dad drove me to Walmart to buy blankets, plastic bins, towels, and all the necessities a college freshman would need. I went from being nervous to being excited about leaving! I was counting down the days. I was in between my grandmother's house and my sister Ashley's place. How cool is that, me still being in high school, but having the freedom to spend time at my sister's place that is only one year older than me. We would order pizza, my mom would fry her famous chicken wings, make homemade fries, and we invited friends over. Those were some of the best times, but I knew I would soon have to leave it all behind.

As my senior year is ending, it is time to get my prom dress, choose a hairstyle, and print my flyers for the yearbook. I am not one to seek attention, but I was voted to run for prom queen. So why not go out with a bang. For some reason, I do not like to be in the spotlight, but I also cannot help the fact that my accomplishments on the track are putting me out there.

I did not win prom queen, but I did leave Palmetto High School with record-breaking times, a better reputation, and a full-ride scholarship to an accredited four-year university.

Part II: Use your Weapons

The College Girl

Within the next couple of weeks, I packed my belongings. I put most of my clothes in boxes so that we could ship them to Kentucky. The only thing I was taking on the plane were two suitcases. It finally dawned on me that I was officially done with high school! I guess this is what it feels like to be an adult and be out on your own. As I look back and reflect on my childhood and high school career, I cannot help but think about everything I had gone through. A lot has happened over the years but through it all, I am grateful. Everyone else is excited about attending college or moving out of their parents' house, but I feel uneasy about it. One minute I am happy and excited; the next minute I am questioning everything in my life. I think the indecisiveness comes from me thinking I do not deserve better. As if I was not hard-working or worthy. As painful as it is to leave my family in Florida, I know it is for the better. Before my dad picked me up from Grandma Dora's house, everyone gathered around to see me off while we snacked on pizza. The whole family was there and guess who else was at grandma's house; Chico. We were serious at this point and made a promise to never leave each other's side in spirit and to always be there for one another. It was hard. By the time my dad arrived in his big truck, everyone was in tears!

The time finally came when I arrived at the Nashville airport. My new teammates were there waiting with big smiles on their faces. I settled in at the brand-new dorm, New Richmond Hall, and unpacked my things. My roommate was not there when I arrived, but she arrived shortly after. She walked in with her mom, grandmother, younger sister, and introduced herself. It was perfect! We had so much in common; I still remember reaching out to shake her hand and noticing her long decorative nails. Some had candy wrappers on them while others were covered with diamonds. Taylor is her name but back in her hometown, they called her, "Tay Tay." Her side of the room was already set up; zebra print pillows with a dash of bright pink here and there. I still had some work to do. Compared to her, I was Plain Jane. I bought a comforter from Walmart and added a few white and lime green pillows to make my bed look nice. Our room was just what I had imagined, cute, girly, and made specifically for us.

Later that evening we heard about our first party, but I was not going. I made up in my mind that I was going to be focused no matter what, so I sat this one out. Oh, but that following week, after doing some soul-searching and realizing that college is also supposed to be fun, I had my outfit ready. It was our first week of practice, not so much running but signing paperwork, team photos, and learning the workout regime. So, I decided to go out. Little did I know, the same pair of cute jeans I put on with that black half vest would later embarrass me. My song came on, the beat dropped, I dropped it low to the floor and the next thing I know, I am running to the bathroom with a big rip in the back of my jeans. The whole basketball and football team was there; I was so ashamed. I ran back to the dorm and called it a night. My teammates could not stop laughing; it had to be the funniest thing ever to them. How embarrassing! I was going to leave that part out of the story, but that is what I get for wearing good ol' faithful. That is what I call a pair of jeans you can throw on for any occasion, and they would make your butt pop if you know what I mean. Listing to Juvenile, 'Back That Thang Up,' I dropped it a lil' too low, and before you know it, I felt some air hit my butt, and I knew it was over. Ah, the memories. I gathered myself together after that party so that I was ready to start the semester the following week.

I am now a freshman in college, and it is everything I once dreamed of. Okay, that was a lie. I am nervous, I have never been away from home like this, I do not know how to cook, and I am wondering how I will get around the city without a car. Hopefully, I will get along with the girls on the track team. We did what was considered the usual, I guess. We took team pictures and then went over to see what the off-campus housing looked like. Everyone who was older on the team had the privilege of living in an apartment, which I thought was cool. The older girls accepted us (the freshman) like we were their younger siblings. They invited us over to the first house party and of course, I did not want to go, but then my roommate reminded me that it was okay to get out a little. Besides, I needed a re-do after the mishap I had at the first official party of the year. At the time, I called myself being in love with my high school sweetheart, Chico. Knowing that I messed up so many times in the past by either sabotaging the relationship or not being faithful, I wanted to do it right this time. I think it was more than puppy love, even if no one else did. I looked at Chico's picture, which sat on my desk, and decided to hang out. So, I got dressed, borrowed my roommates' bright pink colored earrings, and headed out the door. We waited downstairs in front of the lobby entrance of our dorm for the other girls to pick us up. They came quickly, honking the horn, laughing, and full of energy. I admired every one of them. I was wondering if my body would be like theirs by my junior year and if my muscles would be as defined as theirs were.

This party was their welcoming party for the incoming freshman, no boys allowed. It was just my girls and me. It was perfect! Pizza and lots of laughs is what the night consisted of. I felt like I had a team of sisters and my roommate was pretty much a clone of me. From the time her family left that dorm room, we became family. The bond she had with her family was beautiful to witness. She was very close to her family, and when I saw her trying to hold back the tears as they drove away from the dorm, I knew we had to stick together. We had no choice. We went from sharing Ramen noodles to sharing memories we would never forget.

Especially when I split my pants in front of everyone. Now that we got the party out of the way, it was time for the serious stuff; school.

Besides public speaking and theatre, I liked my classes. I thought I wanted to major in Forensic Science until I attended my first Chemistry and Biology lecture. Thank God, they allowed us to change majors within the first couple of weeks of registering. Just when you thought you could be like the actors from your favorite show, Law and Order, reality hits you right in the face. I quickly changed my major to Criminal Justice and chose Social Work as my minor. Between trying to balance the relationship I brought over from high school, getting cleared from exercise-induced asthma, and learning how to take notes effectively, freshman year was looking good. It was almost as good as the male basketball and football players were looking. I am joking, but goodness it is hard to stay focused at times with so much freedom and minimal supervision. I guess this is what everyone was talking about. The college life, where some can stay focused and others, well they tend to stay a few more years than intended because of lack of focus. Classes were somewhat of an extension to what I had learned in high school, they called those prerequisites. I was not complaining, that just meant I still had time to change my major.

I met people from all over. It is a must when you need notes from someone, and the professor says a quiz is quickly approaching. We have a meal card to swipe for breakfast, lunch, and dinner at the Café; Winslow is what it was called. The food was okay, but food is food, and I used to pretend like we were at a five-star restaurant. I was asking my teammates what they felt like eating, every day. Even though the meals were somewhat the same, we made do with what we had. In the meantime, I was getting connected with so many random people. Some funny, some weird, and some cool, but I did not care. I was just excited to meet new people. College is fun, people are going to be different, so I am trying something new and not being antisocial like I was my first few years of high school.

One day, I was called down to the stadium where the coach and the trainers had some bad news. What could possibly go wrong after splitting my pants at the first big party in college? He said I was not cleared to run. I asked him to explain because I did not understand. He said I could not practice until I was cleared by a physician for having exercise-induced asthma. I knew it; I knew it would all come back on me one day. Throughout my entire high school track career, I took a chance, believing that if this is what the man above wants then I will be fine. In college, it was a more serious matter. This had to be one of the most depressing moments in my life. The one thing I have grown to love; I would have to put on the back burner for a while. The one thing I was looking forward to doing every day would now become second place to everything else.

For the following nine months, or so, I had to attend practice and watch from the sidelines, while waiting for the approval to run. Throughout that time, I gained a new meaning to the word patience. Then I began to get homesick, I could not stand to see pictures of my family hanging on my dorm room wall. Not to mention, the freshman fifteen was something I experienced as well. I went from weighing in at 130 to now being 145. This was not good for the sport I was competing in. I went through the motions, pretending like everything was okay. Every day I put on the show and continued to focus on school. I still cannot believe I got stuck in a public speaking class, how terrifying. I never thought I would have to stand in front of an entire class and give a speech on different topics. That was a first. After being shy in both elementary and middle school for not being able to comprehend words, I find myself trying to help others see things from my point of view. I finished the semester strong, anticipating the time when I would be able to compete again. Now it is time to put on my big girl pants, I needed to learn from my freshman year and take those lessons into the next year.

I met a girl named Lindsey, she was always so vibrant and willing to lend a helping hand with no questions asked. I could not be more grateful. She is someone who would stop everything just to make sure you were okay. One day, I needed a ride to and from the airport, and everyone seemed to be in class. Sure enough, I called her, and she was right there to pick me up. I watched how she saved her money each month by separating her spending money from her bill money. At first, I did not understand, but later, it made sense once I received my funds from the school. Money management was important, but what was most significant about her was her faith. In exchange for her doing me favors she would invite me over for mid-day bible studies. It was also my first time ever seeing someone make homemade nachos. Just in case you are wondering, it was not fancy, but it was good, and we were college students. Lindsey would take the Tostito chips and cover them with a handful of cheese, stick them in the microwave for a few seconds and boom! There you have it, homemade nachos.

Everything was good, but sometimes my spirit was off. I felt so far away from God that I questioned if I deserved his love and grace. Especially all those times when I partied and drank until I could not drink anymore during my sophomore and junior year. I was trying to suppress the pain, only to be left with another void I could not feel. Lindsey prayed with me and for me. Those bible studies were life-changing. I have been a part of several cliques growing up and had many friends, but this one did not want anything in return but for me to experience the love of Christ. She was trying to set me free, but, at the time, I wanted to remain trapped. If I could turn back the hands of time, I would have run through that open door sooner. Lindsey did not waver in her faith, she kept believing that I would change, and she saw something in me that I could not see in myself. Until this day, I wonder what it was that led her to be so persistent in wanting to help me grow spiritually. I also asked myself this question: will I ever be as strong as a Christian as she is? This was the start of my faith walk, my Christian experience, and my journey with The Lord.

Although Lindsey was the first to introduce me to my Savior, I was not very receptive. It was not long before Mariah, a girl on the basketball team, started to have her very own bible study with both the track girls and basketball team. She was the Most Valuable Player (MVP) on the team during that time. She was known for holding the team together and shooting three-pointers. I had people around me who were believers, but it was only my sophomore year, and I had just starting drinking, and no I am not talking about Kool-Aid. I am talking about that other stuff. The stuff that had me doing jumping jacks in the middle of the apartment while everyone counted to see just how long I could go before I got tired and "could not feel my tongue." It is funny to think I touched a drink after saying I would never do that or do drugs. I never liked the feeling of not being in total control. When I drank, it felt like my yes and my no was compromised. It was weird because I hate the taste, but I kept drinking. I ran to those double-red cups every time life got hard.

At some point during my sophomore year, I begin to finally get the hang of things, the girls on the track team said things get better as you become familiar with college life. Knowing that, I am feeling more and more like a college student each day. After a long and stressful freshman year, away from the track, I am cleared! Hallelujah! That only took forever. I was hungrier than I have ever been to run. I could not wait to join my teammates on the track and in the weight room. It felt like my first day of school all over again. I was filled with joy and excitement! Now, I felt like a college athlete. Everything is going great, practices are consistent, I am getting some muscle definition for the first time, and my body is starting to transform the way it needs to.

It was another ordinary day in Murray, KY and my teammates and I were walking out to do our warm-up lap. We stretched and did our normal routine in the grass, and then it was time for the track workout. One thing about collegiate track practice is that the warm-up always felt like a mini workout in my opinion. It was nothing like high school. It is tire pull day, yes, we are pulling car tires across the football field with a strap around our waist. It was easy for me. Practice is over, and I look at the coach, he glances back at me, and I tell him I am feeling good, and he asks,

"So, do you have one more in you?" Being one of the three new girls on the team, I say, "Yep, I sure do!" I take off, low angles, the tire bouncing up and down across the field, I am at top end speed and pop! There goes my hamstring, halfway through the exercise. Talk about pain, I was in shock. Something I never expected to happen. This was my first introduction to the rehab and training room. I was out for the rest of the season.

After waking up each morning, walking to the training room at 5am to get in the ice bathe, I was ready to be done. Some days were better than others, and after a while, I could practice on it a little but was told to take it easy. After building some strength, I could compete in a few races but nothing spectacular, no record-breaking times, which was my goal. A few 3rd and 4th place finishes here and there, but I was not impressed with my sophomore year. Toward the end of the season, I started to party and drank a little more. Also, I met a guy on the football team. At this point, things had fizzled out between my HS sweetheart and me. While still being focused on school, I felt myself being a bit freer if you will.

The end of the year was approaching, and there was a rumor going around saying that our coach would not be around much longer. Well, that rumor ended up being true. So, what now? Fear started to creep in. I began to think about my decision. Did I make a mistake by coming to this college or is this just another part of life? Moreover, I was starting to use most of my Pell grant money I had saved. So, I decided to apply for a job on campus where most of the girls on the team worked. Racerthon, we worked a couple of hours soliciting donations from alumni in different backgrounds and fields. It was fun, and I could use the extra cash. I remember speaking with Matt Kelly, he was that one person that all the athletes confided in and went to whenever there was a problem. I will never forget this, he looked at me with a serious face and said, "Do not leave Alexis, we are going to find a good coach, trust me." I took his advice, and I stayed.

Not really knowing how everything was going to turn out, I was still looking forward to my junior year in college. Where did the time go? The girl, who was just competing at the state championship in Florida, is now a junior in college. Talk about life changing. After being in a small room without a kitchen, I was looking forward to off-campus housing. On the track team, I was now considered one of the upperclassmen and was now going to move to an apartment to make room for the incoming freshman on the team. My roommate's name was Lexie, how ironic, but she was a pole vaulter. We would make jokes about being called Lex1 and Lex2. I loved her spirit. She is one of those girls that is smart, kind, and just liked to have fun while making others happy. I remember her coming home every 3 weeks or so with a new hair color. We always tried to guess what color she would have next. Lexie had a turquoise two-door car, overall, she just stood out. She was the only girl I knew with crazy piercings and a loud sound system in her car. I used to tell her that she was a black girl at heart. Between spending time with Lexie and Patrick, the guy on the football team, I was happy. Patrick was a different type of guy. His dreadlocks attracted me to him. Girls from Florida are known to talk to guys with dreadlocks and tattoos. Pat is from New Orleans and loves him some good ol' soul food and pancakes made just how his grandma makes them. I was excited to get to know him.

A few weeks passed, and the track team got an email saying they found a new coach. Matt Kelly kept his promise to me, and the athletic department did their job. It was now time for us to go and meet the new head coach and assistant. I was open-minded and positive; I knew things had to get better. We went from not having a coach to having two coaches. The head coach was Jenny Severns. Some gave her the title of being the long-distance coach, but no, she was the coach, the boss lady. Although she spent most of her time with the distance runners, she knew what it took to win. Long distance was her specialty, but she was beyond committed to the team. As our distance runners were leaning across the finish line, so was she, with her stopwatch. She was super funny, but she also meant business. She made sure everything was in place, we had all the equipment we needed, and that we set a good example when we went out to represent the team. We knew, if you were called into her office, then it was either for an award or something else. That something else was not always pleasant. I learned a lot from Coach Jenny. She taught me how to make sacrifices and that it was not always about me. She expressed the importance of always giving your best no matter what. She pushed me passed my limits, and as the head coach, you could count on her to run around the track with you while you are competing. Yes, she was one of those coaches. I literally felt like she ran every 4x4 relay with me. I am glad she was placed in my path.

Then we have the assistant Coach Keisler or Coach K. He was unique in his coaching style, and he knew his stuff. In our first meeting, I got the feeling he had a plan before I even thought of one. He asked me about freshman and sophomore year then about my goals for this upcoming season. I explained that I was not able to compete almost my whole freshman year and my sophomore year started off strong until my hamstring injury. Now, I feel like I am behind the other girls. I felt like I was a nobody and coming from being the fastest female in my hometown, this was very upsetting. He responded, "What do you want to achieve this year?" Trying to keep the tears from falling… I told him I wanted them to know my name, and by them I meant coaches, athletes, and the whole world. I told him I wanted to walk into a building and have them know me before I introduced myself. He said, "okay, it is a done deal." As if it was easy and a part of his plan the whole time.

At this point, I had nothing to lose but a lot to gain. I was committed. Fall training was around the corner, the semester has started, and everything is off to a great start. I am getting stronger. More focused than ever, I have a good relationship with my coaches, but the only thing I did not know was that being better would require 2x the effort. At one point, because of my crazy 18-hour class schedule, I had to practice in the morning without the team. Just me, coach, and the wet track. The track was always damp after the snow melted. I enjoy running by myself but, then again, I would rather be challenged by my teammates. However, the thought of being my only competition pushed me mentally. The indoor season started, I was one of the strongest on the team. I had the fastest splits in practice, and I mastered stadium runs. A split is the time it takes you to get from one marked location on the track to the next. In the middle of our training schedule, we had a few people join the team. It was always exciting to welcome new teammates! Before I go any further, I want to share a quick story about one of my indoor track meets. I ran at Notre Dame all by my lonesome. Well Sharda, another girl on the team, was there to run the hurdles. It was a cold morning, and we were there to qualify for Indoor Nationals at the Last Chance meet. I warmed up to run the 60m dash and ran a personal best but did not qualify in that event, so I decided to take a shot at the 200m. It was time to check in, 1st call, 2nd call, and then, final call; I was the only one standing on the starting line ready to go. Originally, I was in a lower lane, but the official said I could choose whichever lane I liked if I was going to go ahead and run the race, so I chose lane 4, that is my favorite number. The gun went off, once again, I was in the zone. I could not hear anything until the race was over. I remember Coach Brown, from Austin Peay telling me, "Lex it's just you and the clock." That was all the motivation I needed to hear. That day, I earned my lane and was on my way to participate at the 2012 indoor Championships, in Idaho.

Still being new at this whole college captain thing, I had taken on the role of showing the new girls around and keeping them on the right track. This started to happen around the end of my sophomore year. After sitting out my freshman year and returning stronger the following year, I earned a new responsibility. The girls somewhat gravitated toward me, and the coaches encouraged it. With this new role became new responsibilities, but I was ready to take on the challenge. Leading by example, I started to break records that were more than a decade old and then turned around and broke my own records. Things were moving along quickly, I was starting to have media interviews before and during practice, but I remained humbled. I was addicted to success, winning was not enough, I wanted more.

Indoor season was coming to an end and I am already doing better than I had ever imagined. I had a routine where I would go to morning weights, attend classes, volunteer at Need Line and the animal shelter, go to study hall, run at our second practice for the day, then head to work. I was working two jobs going into the outdoor season. Shortly after Christmas break, I started to work for the on-campus housing department as a security guard for the dorms. I worked the midnight shift, 12am until 8am. I would sleep for a few hours then go to work. It was not so bad once I was on schedule or at least that is what I told myself. I know it probably seemed crazy looking in from the outside. College athlete on a full-ride scholarship, working two jobs, but I always had a fear of being broke or in debt. Living off-campus, it was hard trying to find a ride to the store outside of catching the bus. I was working two jobs because I wanted to save up for a down payment on a car.

I believe the struggle can make or break you. I channeled all my energy into applying force on the track. It worked for me! I put in the work, and everything else took care of itself. Murray State is a part of the Ohio Valley Conference and during those championships Coach K always reminded me of our talk. He pushed me to reach my full potential. He knew me as an athlete and as a person, and I think that is what strengthens a coach-athlete relationship. It was the OVC outdoor championships, spring of 2012. I ran both the 100m and 200m dash along with anchoring the 4x1 and 4x4 relay. 1st place across the board and I qualified for the U.S. Olympic Trials! I had no idea. I remember being nervous but ready to compete the whole day. I did the same exact thing before every race: stretch, listen to music, then say a prayer. I always wore my cheap socks I bought from the dollar store, navy blue with a grey design on them. Someone once said they looked like old church socks, but I did not care. It was either those or my red, white and blue USA socks. The socks were significant to me because they taught me a life lesson. Although they were cheap, I believed I could do the impossible with those socks on. To me, my socks were equivalent to the special water in the movie, Space Jam. I knew I had won the 100m dash, but I did not know my time until it was announced. I can still hear the announcer on the loudspeaker. Everyone stood still, waiting for the results, "…and our 1st place finisher, with a time of 11.28 seconds, Alexis Love!" That is a stadium record and automatic standard for the U.S. Olympic Trials. It did not hit me right away; I could not believe what I had just heard. Out of nowhere someone comes from behind and throws the Gatorade bucket of water on Coach K's head. I was hyped, energized, and pumped to run the 200-meter final. Usually, I feel like I am out of gas but not that day, I was ready! It is the start of the 200, the gun goes off, and I can feel myself ahead of the pack, crossing the finish line and again, another 1st place finish. Another automatic time to run in the U.S. team trials. It did not feel real. I was in denial. After the awards ceremony on the track, we drove back to Murray, and of course, the track team celebrated that night. My social media pages were going crazy; it took me forever to respond back to everyone who wished me well. It was such a good feeling.

Sharda was always there. She would call herself my personal cheerleader, and that she was. She was one of those little sisters you could not get away from. Lexie was my roommate on the official lease, but you might as well say Sharda's name was on there as well. After things did not work out with Pat, I was down and depressed most of the time. I must say; the end of our relationship was mostly my fault but then we both came to an agreement and decided to move on. Sharda would stop by the apartment unannounced; she would walk straight to my room and stand in front of me and be goofy until I decided to smile. It is almost like she shared my pain with me. She understood that I just needed a shoulder to cry on. I needed a friend to be there even if I thought they were annoying. Looking back, I realize I was just a little too serious. We grew closer and closer as time passed by. We took trips together; attended Mariah's bible studies together, and even planned a summer cruise. Sharda, my first roommate Taylor, and I went on a cruise to the Bahamas before the 2012 U.S. Olympic Trials.

The cruise was planned months before. I received one of those automated recordings saying I won a vacation cruise. After making sure everything was legit, I paid a small fee, and we were all set to go. At that price, I was going, I did not believe in getting rest. My thing was, I worked hard and had good grades, so it was time to reward myself. My dad says it is always good to reward yourself even if it is something small. Well, in this case, it was go hard or go home. Sharda was that friend I was looking for my whole life. Someone to make me crawl out of my shell, someone to cry with and someone to be goofy with. It always made sense as to why she was always excited about her theatre class, she was a character, but she was my friend! Oh, how I love Sharda.

After returning from the cruise, it was time to pack and head out to Eugene, Oregon for the Olympic Trials. "The Road to London," is what the banner reads. Sharda drove me to the stadium where Coach K and Coach Jenny were waiting for me. I was calm until the plane took off down the runway; that is when I knew my dreams were becoming a reality.

We arrived at the hotel, nothing too fancy, but I was not focused on that anyway. I just wanted to drop my bags off and relax. Once I was settled in, I made sure to get on my knees and give the Lord a huge thank you. I mean c'mon, I literally went from being a nobody to a somebody, and I cannot take credit for that. There had to be some supernatural strength and speed coming from above. Coach Jenny and Coach K made sure I had everything I needed for the trip. For ten days straight, it was the same routine. We woke up to eat breakfast, I did my shakeout, which most of the time consisted of running around the hotel or in the hall if it was too cold outside. Then I returned to the room for a full day of rest. Track can be boring on the days we have downtime or no competition. Depending on the location of the race, it can take days or a full week to get acclimated to the weather. Eventually the time came to get my credentials, and the only thing I could think about was to just smile and not look nervous around the professional athletes. Walking into the room to pick up my gifts and get my photo taken was the moment that gave me a sense of belonging. For the first time in a long time, I felt like my hard work had paid off. Just being there was enough to cause me to have a panic attack, but I managed to find my happy place. My happy place was relaxing while watching Law and Order. There was no pressure because I was going into the meet with this in mind, "I cannot lose." I can only come out a winner. The last sprinter from Murray State to compete in the trials was Heather Samuel, back in 1994. My goal was to beat her records. I was successful in some but was not able to break her 100-meter time of 11.20 seconds.

The days were dragging by as if time was at a standstill and I was in one of those old Western movies. Okay, that may be a little dramatic, but that is exactly what I felt at the time. As race day was approaching, there were times where I had to turn my phone completely off so there were no distractions. I had never received so many phone calls and text messages in my life. What an honor! Little ol' me, from Palmetto, FL running was with other World Class Sprinters. Leading up to the race, I did my normal routine. I woke up to eat breakfast and did a quick run through the hotel hallway while stretching in my room. Then I rested for a while until it was time to put on my uniform and head to the track.

I was never the type to be flashy or make myself known. When I arrived, my coaches and I found a quiet corner, so I could be alone. My motto was "When I step foot on the track, this is when I will be seen." After sitting for an hour or two, it was time to warm up. My warm-up consisted of running a lap, stretching, and finishing with drills. By this time, I am sweating and ready to go. As I take a sip of water and proceed to the check-in tent, my adrenaline starts to pump. After checking in for the third time, the runners are required to stay in a secured area until their heat is called out. The Official yelled out my heat, I stood up, grabbed my belongings and now, it was show time. We walked out onto the track, myself and the other professional athletes, I was one of the youngest. We were all introduced on national television and the start time was less than five minutes away. Next thing you know, I am on the track, in the set position, feet on the starting blocks and ready to run my heart out.

The gun goes off, the race is underway, and I soar to the front in 3rd place making it to the semifinals in the 100-meter dash while being the only collegiate runner in that heat. A few days later, I approached the 100-meter semifinal with the same effort, but this time I let the weather get to me. This was all new to me, the whole warm-up process in the cold weather. I had never performed on such a big stage where security takes you to the back moments before your race. Sitting in the call room, I tried to do my best to stay warm, but I could feel myself losing that fire I had during the prelims. Nonetheless, I was ready to compete. The race starts, and this time I can feel the wet track, I can see and hear the crowd and before you know it the race is over. What was different? I was not completely focused and locked in. I was very disappointed in myself, but after a talk with the coaches, they reminded me that I had another shot. I am thankful for the break in between runs because I needed to gather myself both mentally and physically for the 200 meters. The day came where I had to leave it all on the line again, holding nothing back. I made it to the semifinals in the 200-meter as well, but that is where my Olympic journey came to an end.

Everything seemed so surreal. It felt like I was watching myself do some incredible things and could not believe it was happening in real life. The stadium was empty, the track was clear, and the rain was gone. It was time to return home, to Murray. I did not respond to messages or tweets until I had time to process my experience, which was about a week later. I made it back to Murray safely, and none other than Sharda Bettis is there waiting for me with a big smile on her face as if she had just won the lotto. She was so proud of me. She called me her WCS which stood for World Class Sprinter. She said I was still the best in her eyes. It had not hit me until weeks later that I, Alexis Love, had just run in the 2012 U.S. Olympic Trials. I ended the season being the Ohio Valley Conference (OVC) 100m and 200m champion. I was the indoor OVC 200m champion, 9x OVC Athlete of the year, OVC Track athlete of the year, 3x USTFCCCA All-American, 4x qualifier for the NCAA Division 1 East Regional, NCAA Division 1 100m finalist, and ranked top 25 in the USA in the indoor 200m. I cannot complain at all. I had one goal, and that was to make a name for myself. My mission was accomplished.

God, I just want to say thank you! Thank you for everything. I can remember back in high school when I used to sit at home in my room, classroom, or wherever and write to You. The whole time I thought it was just my diary, but I knew it had another purpose. I knew You were the only one that understood everything I was going through. I might have been too young then but, I know now that You had a positive plan and purpose for my life. I can sit here and smile when I think about it. You allowed me to go through those things because You knew I could handle it; You knew it would make me a stronger person. Look at me today; I know You are proud of me. I just want to say thank you, again! You did not have to give Your one and only son to die for my sins. You brought me so far. Here I am, in Murray, KY at 7:58 pm, on a Saturday night, writing a love letter to You. Just overwhelmed with joy and I know that I will be okay. The tears will not stop, but I know You have a reason for all the things that are happening in my life at this moment. Wow, I am about to be a senior in college next year. I am almost there, Lord. Thank you for everything. I could not be more thankful for my blessings. I just want to be closer to You. Sometimes I get on my knees and cry, but You know why without me saying a word. You know what I need, and You have proven that time after time. I trust You.

Moving forward to my senior year, everything was so different from the trials regarding the recognition I received on campus. The interviews doubled, professors called me out in the middle of lecture; I was known as the "track star" but this time on a larger scale. I remember walking into study hall when Matt Kelly asked me, "Is it harder to get to the top or stay at the top?" I thought it was a trick question, so I paused for a second, but it was a simple answer. I responded, "oh it was hard to get there for sure, now I only have to do it all over again." No stress. I was feeling good and at a happy place in my life. Nothing could stop me. I was more committed to track than ever. Almost every day of the new semester I was reminded of my recent accomplishments at the trials. I made it. I could relax a little, so I thought.

By this time, I am heading in the right direction to graduate, I am meeting with professors after hours and staying on top of my game. As I mentioned earlier, I decided to major in Criminal Justice and minor in Social Work. My professor, Dr. Merianos, said it was strange because she had never met someone who wanted to lock up bad guys then help restore families at the same time. I guess I did not think of it that way. I never wanted to retaliate or seek justice for what happened to me in the early years of my life. I only wanted an explanation and understanding. I asked Dr. Merianos if I could meet with her to go over a review for the test and of course, she said yes. Somehow while discussing the next lesson, I ended up telling her my life story. What a relief it was to have someone like her sympathize with me. I will always love her for that. She is the kind of person that allows you to be yourself, unfiltered. Right there in her office, I broke down crying; I let go and before you knew it my face was covered as if someone threw water on me. I had so many questions for my professor. First, why did she care so much? Second, why did she make time to listen to my story? Third, why was she inclined to help me? I may not get these questions answered but the time spent was necessary. After that meeting, I was sure that she was labeled my favorite professor of all time.

The next day, I felt rejuvenated in practice, but there was a shift in my thought process. I started to feel a weight on my shoulders. I tried to keep a leveled head, but I knew everyone was expecting me to do the same thing I did last season. I was still the team captain, so I could not let my teammates down, I must practice what I preach, and I know I cannot let my family down either. It all just seems to be too much. I feel myself shutting down, not wanting to be around anyone and the only time I felt better was when I attended church. Pastor Catlett and his wife always made the track team feel welcome. I decided to join the choir so that I would spend more time being involved with activities at the church and would feel less of a desire to want to party. God has been too good to me for me to go back to how I used to be. Lost, drinking at every party, trying to hide the pain, and not knowing my self-worth was all bad.

Indoor season is about to start, and I know I need to be focused to do what I did last season or even better. I am not sure what is wrong with me, but I have been in and out of it lately. One day I am okay and the next I feel like I am losing before I even start the race. Of course, the days were not all bad, but I felt like I could always do better. That is not a good feeling to have either because you cannot rerun the race. Here I am, walking to my last class of the day. It was one of my interesting courses, child abuse class. I am so close to taking my afternoon nap that I can feel the warmth of my fluffy leopard comforter. My cell phone rings just as I am walking into class and it is my sister. I answered, and there was a long pause on the other end. I said hello for the second time, and I hear her murmur under her breath, "Mama knows." I lost it, ran out of the building and started to have somewhat of a panic attack, I was in shock. She said one conversation led to another and she ended up telling her. My first thought was drama, drama, and more drama. Just when everything was going well for me, well kind of, this happens. I had to think of something quick to tell Coach K in practice because I knew I was going to be all over the place mentally. I tried to explain but at the end of the day I am there on a full-ride scholarship to run, and he is there to do his job. This was one of those suck it up and be strong moments. The time when you cannot wait to get back to your room, so you can cry it out. A long hard, ugly cry just that one night, to get it all out was much needed.

At this point, the indoor season is pretty much coming to an end, and I am anticipating the outdoor season even more. Everyone looks to the outdoor season because indoor session is only from December to February, very short. The outdoor season is more my thing, because the weather is better, and I am in my element. Growing up in Florida, you must love the sunny weather during track season. I have had success here and there, but nothing like last season's record-breaking moments. Things are not so bad all around, I mean my grades are good, I am in the process of being a part of the best sisterhood there is, and I have a car. Days go by and every time my phone rings, my heart skips a beat because I know the day will come when I must explain some things to my mom. So much for a smooth senior year, huh? Well maybe it will not be too bad, maybe I can consider talking to the counselors here on campus, but then again, I will just call Ms. Moyer. Somehow, some way, she always knows exactly what to say to make me feel better. I know the Lord did not bring me this far to leave me. I know He has a plan for me.

My nights are getting longer, I feel like I have not slept in days, and on track, it is almost as if I am going through the motions. Now, I am just trying to finish the semester strong. Kind of ready for everything to be over with. My time at Murray State is expiring. Soon, I will be graduating with my bachelor's degree in the Spring of May 2013. I talked to Meagan about possibly doing a 5th year or my masters here, but I changed my mind. The sad part about this whole thing is that I do not want to stay here or go back home to Florida. I received a call last week from a coach in Texas, maybe I will take him up on that offer to train and live there as a professional athlete. I do not know much about professional track, but it sounds good so far. Not to mention I will continue working at Racer Thon, so I am not too stressed about money and being able to buy my own cap and gown. Racer Thon was my part-time job on campus. I have been doing well at saving these past two years. The hours at work do not bother me anymore, but I remember when it made me feel nauseated because I could not get a full eight hours of sleep in.

The finish line is here, I finished the track season healthy; not with the best times, but I am grateful for the opportunity. My family will be driving up soon to see me walk across the stage. I hope everyone gets along and it is a nice turnout. That is all I ever wanted, a big happy family. Maybe it is true, maybe I do believe in fairy tales. I am eager to see what the next part of my life looks like. The real deal, the grown-up part when you are out on your own. It is now time to leave the dorms, parties, sleepless nights, and untold love stories behind. You know the untold stories I am talking about. The ones where you thought you were in love. The ones where you were sure about marrying the football player because you learned how to make pancakes just like his grandma. The stories I could not wait to share with my teammates only to cry over them later. All in all, I had fun in college. From the long nights studying and trying to make a miracle appear while writing a ten-page paper overnight. I cannot do much complaining; the campus life was great. It was where I learned a hundred ways to make Ramen Noodles taste like a 5-star meal. Now it is time to put on my pointy toe heels and walk into the next phase of my life with expectancy. God is in control. I am a big girl now, no more daddy's little girl.

Welcome to the Real World

Sometimes you must eliminate people from your life to grow. Who knew what the real world really had to offer? I thought high school was the real world. At the time, it sure as heck felt like my whole entire life and reputation was built on my high school career. I have learned not to waste energy regretting the way things of the past or thinking about what could have happened. Instead of running away from my problems, I welcome them with open arms now. Well not so much, but you get the idea.

The Road to Recovery

God, most of my prayers have been answered. I do believe with all things through Christ You will strengthen me.

I realize that we will search for answers that will never bring us closure, and we may have questions that will never get answered, but you must find out your why. When I wrote down my whys, it made me that much more determined to be a winner. It stems from my childhood. Sometimes, I feel like I could have had more or maybe even done less to not mess up my reputation as a teenager. I dug deep into a box I swore I would never open once it was closed. It was like that chest full of toys that my dad had when I was six years old, but instead, I locked it and threw away the key. Of course, it was not a chest full of toys I am talking about, it is a heart full of pain and angst. A heart seeking closure. After jumping over that hurdle and learning why I was so bitter and hurt all the time, I wanted to know how I could fix my heart. It is one thing to identify the problem, but the real discovery is found in the solution to the problem. After dissecting my life in chronological order, I have concluded that it is not my job to try to put all the pieces together. Let alone, try to figure this masterpiece out on my own.

Leave the whys of the past alone and get to the whys of the present. Ask relevant questions that will help you in the present. I believe that if I can figure out what is triggering certain thoughts, then I can work towards having a better future. I am pretty much done beating myself up about what I did in the past. People will always remember the bad and forget to mention the good you do. Again, another why I Running for My Life will never have the answer to. All in all, I know I had to go through those things as a child so that I would one day have a story. The biggest why I would like to know is why I am here and what on earth my purpose is since God saw fit to keep me in this world. It must be something bigger than I could ever imagine because what I have seen and heard is by far the craziest things I have experienced. The homelessness I used to see while riding the bus to school, violence in the streets, drugs, you name it, and I have seen it. I am so thankful to have made it out. Who would have ever thought that little ol' me, Alexis Love, would grow up to be a professional runner, after all the things that have happened in my past? Even in high school, I had enough drama to fill a high school cafeteria. It was nobody but the Lord that was on my side. I would like to think that it is over, the hardship that is, but if I am not in one trial that means another is not too far around the corner. I try so hard to think positive, but the struggle is all I know. Maybe one day, this too will change.

"God, thank You for making me as You have. Help me to discover the gifts You have planted inside of me. Inspire me to invest in them. Help me to enjoy what I turn my hand to. And to work at everything as if I am doing it for You."

A Lost Soul

I have tried many things, only to be left with a void I could not fill. It was all an illusion, a temporary pleasure that would lead me back to the one place I tried to avoid: the dark side. My longing and desire was to be closer to God. When I thought I was in love, it was a no. When I thought I was ready to be an adult, it was a no. For example, once I got to high school, I began to use my looks to get what I wanted. No was not a word in my vocabulary. Everything was a yes, the material things, the money came fast, getting my nails and hair done was never a concern, and it was all a part of my plan. I guess you can say I was used to getting what I wanted. It is almost like I was asking to be hurt because I could not believe a man could be loving and trustworthy. I dated the same type of men, repeatedly looking for different results; it never happened. I believe you are what you attract. I was a hurt individual connecting with other people who were hurting. Now I realize the demand and the respect for a queen is what I deserved the whole time. Of course, I did not figure this out on my own. It took numerous accounts of feeling down about myself and the decisions I made in life to get my attention.

We need different people in our lives that we can trust to be open with us. To get us to see the bigger picture and find solutions when we are at a dead end. For a long time, I fought against what would set me free. Most people would have turned to drugs and crime as a way of coping, I decided to tough it out. Tough situations build tougher individuals. I am thankful for my no's. Every no brought me closer to my yes. Man's rejection was God's protection. Are you not glad that every time someone has let you down, a job did not hire you, or you were told you were not good enough? I am. In those times, I kept the faith because I knew my story had a different ending. Keep smiling, keep believing and the good Lord will turn it around for your good. The best is yet to come!

The Void, it is what we try to avoid. Knowing that it's like a double edge sword. Trying to live my life and be the light to the one I adore. But it's hard to live right while trying to quiet the noise. But of course, we make excuses to justify our sin. But let the truth be told it came from deep within. But I thank God for His word which says He has a plan. If only I could go back to high school when I was young and played in the band. Just to keep my mind off what everyone was saying. Looking left and right trying to fill the void. Screaming no, please stop it, thinking boys will just be boys. Living a life of regret, cold sweats while fighting depression. But at the thought of suicide, I was reminded of His great presence. God is faithful, God is good. I was just misunderstood. A young female lost and hurt. And looking for love. I must admit. I tried to fill the void. Feeling hopeless and doing some soul searching. Realizing my longing was to be close to my Lord.

The violent craving has shown up in my life, time after time. It has controlled me. It was like an urge I could not avoid. It has left me in pain each time. It is always there, and I am never satisfied. Things I reached for were not satisfying. I even tried to fill the void with food. I would eat all the time but was never full. I had money, met men with money, but none of that mattered. I ran, but it never seemed to make me happy. I needed God. I had an appetite for His love. The things we crave are not the things we are hungry for.

Pro Track Life

Murray State University was the right school for me. It brought me friends, great teammates, different coaches, up's and downs, The U.S. Olympic trials, and most importantly, great memories. As I embark on a new journey to become a professional athlete, I realize I had to go through struggles that would prepare me for what is to come. I just want to be great. Above all else, I want to be number one in the world, point blank period.

Lord, here I am in Dallas, Texas, after I decided to take the coach up on his offer. A lot has been going on, and I am not sure which way to turn. I knew moving here would be risky, but I did not factor in what all could go wrong. I know that I must make sacrifices to get to where I want to be on the track, but this is tough. I thought it was going to be easier for whatever reason because I did not have school to think about. Being a student-athlete was challenging. I figured if I got through college then I could make it through anything in life. I could not let this moment pass me by. Having the opportunity to compete as a professional athlete is a dream come true. Living arrangements, issues with my current coach, working two jobs, the list goes on. I feel like I am back at square one. My oldest sister, Cardiena was so kind to let me sleep on her floor with a blow-up mattress and occasionally in her bed when she left town. I do not know where I would be if she was not in Texas. I wish someone would have told me that the pro track life is not all glitz and glam. I am so glad Destiny, a friend from college, invited me into her apartment because I was at the end of my rope. Destiny was a cool down to earth girl that everyone loved at

Murray State. She had long curly dreadlocks and a big white smile. She was someone you could go to about almost anything. She told me the couch was all mine and after sleeping on a blowup mattress at my sister's place, the couch was a step up. Granted, my sister did everything she could to help me, but I understand she is about to have a teenager now. My niece is getting bigger every day and is already taller than me. I realize that it is no one else's responsibility to take care of me. I am an adult now. I should be able to take care of myself, or maybe it is this thing called pride that is getting in the way. I guess you never know how prideful you are until you are faced with a situation that forces you to depend on others. The fact that I would rather work two jobs to make ends meet instead of asking for help says a lot about where I am both mentally and spiritually.

The roads are slippery and wet from the ice, and I have not been outside in three days. I am afraid, but deep down I believe everything will be okay. I just need to remember that God oversees everything and that He is the head of my life. I am working on not letting my circumstances determine how I go about my day. I do wish I could at least make it to my job today, Dick's Sporting Good and Old Navy. Old Navy was not bad at all because I would go in at four in the morning and unload the trucks to get the merchandise ready before the store would open. I never knew how much it took to have those clothing racks look up to date and trends in the latest fashion. I have a new-found respect for anyone who works retail. This job was much different than working customer service at the outlet mall in high school. This job has taught me patience on a whole new level.

Dick's Sporting Good was also a great learning experience. I was given the job title, "footwear specialist." Although it sounded fancy, it was just another way to say I worked in the shoe department. I was appreciative of the managers that worked with my track schedule because that was always hit or miss when applying for jobs. I figured I would be upfront with them so that way there were no surprises when I had to travel for a meet. Some days, I feel as though I cannot lift another shoe box, but I know it is the Lord who gives me strength.

I called Ms. Moyer after work one day because I needed advice. She was always understanding and very caring. I wonder if anyone else keeps in contact with her, but nevertheless, she was always there. She could tell by the tremble in my voice that something was wrong. She said, "Alexis, sweetheart, what seems to be the problem." I told her that I felt like I was losing my mind and the journaling was not helping. I went on to tell her that I felt like my diary entries were haunting me. She took a quick pause and said, "God wants you to let go of a burden." So immediately I thought, yep it is the journals I am holding on to; that was confirmation. I planned to burn my journals for sure after we hung up. She said I should not burn them because God probably wants me to write a book, to tell my story. For the first time, I felt a different way about writing to myself in those stupid journals. I never knew Ms. Moyer was so spiritual until that moment. She knew exactly what to say and at the right time.

It was not long after I decided the two jobs were a strain on my body that I decided to try a temp agency to look for a better job. I had never heard of this before, but it was worth a try. I walked into the interview and was completely honest. I shared with the supervisor that I recently moved to Dallas, Texas to train as a professional runner. I was hesitant about mentioning the days I would be out due to track season, but I did it anyway. Luckily, a week later, I received the phone call I was waiting for. I was hired and expected to start that following Monday! This was a breath of fresh air. It was the beginning of 2014 and the start of having a peace of mind. I went to work the next morning with some sort of peace knowing that my financial stability was going to get better. I quit the two jobs to work this one. My new job was working for a corporate office in Irving, Texas that collected on defaulted payday loans. I was proud of myself because I had managed to work my way up in the company. I was the number one collector because I collected one thousand dollars in one day. A long way from when I first started this job a few months ago, talk about having thick skin, try calling someone to ask for their money after they have already paid their other bills. This job was making me tougher than ever, well at least on the phone. I had some sort of experience while working at the Alumni Center at Murray State, but never anything like this. This was telemarketing on a whole new level. My spirit had to be in check every morning, I am sure that is the only way I would make it through the day. I cannot take full credit; I had an awesome supervisor pushing me to be great every day. He understood sports, so he would use that to motivate me and train me in a way that made sense to me. He was also a "go-getter," but differently, he knew how to get you fired up for the job! That is the kind of energy I needed for the drive home after work.

It was always a one-hour drive to work and the same during rush hour leaving work. Just when I thought I could take a minute to myself, I had one more long drive, and that was to practice. Somehow even with all the traffic, I manage to make it on time. Sometimes I am so exhausted that I can barely roll off Destiny's couch, but I must remember why I am here. Texas is huge, so it does not make a difference if you leave work early or not, you are bound to run into traffic.

My first international meet is coming up in Saskatoon, Canada and I am ecstatic! I met with one of the athletes from Dennis Mitchell's camp, however, I am not sure what to think of this. I heard he is one of the best coaches' around. I will stick it out in Texas until I can work my way up to the top. While attending Murray State, I thought college was my most challenging test of faith. Little did I know the real test would come soon after college. It seemed so easy in college, but now on the professional level, everyone is fast. To reclaim my spot and feel a sense of belonging again, I must give it my all.

Homeless Hotel

This is why they say, "never say never!" I found myself homeless because my friend whom I was living with accepted a job offer and I had within 24 hours to move. With no place to go and no money for a hotel, I found myself riding around with all my belongs in my car. As it started to get dark, I said to myself by midnight I would call Kyle, whom which my family would not approve, but the only person I knew who had space, "not an extra room, just a little space!". He was nice enough to make space in his closet for my clothes and provide a blow-up mattress. To my surprise it was soft and comfortable, truly a step up from a couch. Again, I was truly grateful! Kyle worked a full-time job and traveled often, so we rarely saw one another. His only requirement was I cleaned up my fake hair, LOL. Other than that, it worked out great!

"I am such a happy person when I read and pray more. God knows what is going to happen each day. He will not show me what is ahead, but He will prepare me for the journey."

After working so hard for many years and not having my own, I finally got my own place! I rushed to leave work just so I could get my money order and be at the apartment complex before closing time. After touring the model apartment one last time, I was in awe all over again. It was everything I pictured; a nice, comfy place made just for me. Now, back at the office and going over paperwork it was time to sign on the dotted line and close the deal! I ran out to my car to get my wallet and money order, and on my trip to my vehicle I ran into a lady on a golf cart who stopped me, she told me God wanted me to be still and focus on what He is doing in my life and be free. I did not understand what she meant, so I decided to go the Creator Himself and seek Him for direction in my life. I had so many questions…*God, what do you mean, and how can I be free? Lord, I thank you for speaking to me through this lady. I don't understand this, but I do love You for always looking out for me.*

Having my own place was still surreal. I was so ecstatic about the whole experience of decorating it. I feel as though

I waited long enough, and I worked hard enough. I felt entitled to having everything I once dreamt of. I figured, my friends are getting settled in after graduating, and some already have an apartment or a house. I know everyone's situation is different, but who was more deserving than me. After feeling discouraged at that leasing office for not getting my own place after college, I got in my car and drove off into the sunset. There was nothing to do but trust a stranger and takes God's word for it. It is true when He says He can use anyone because that was one I least expected. Weeks went by, and I was still in doubt. I trusted what the Lord said, but I could not rationalize it, so I kept trying. I called the leasing office one more time and could not believe what I was hearing. I learned the management team was fired for something no one dared to speak on. In the end, the rejection was my protection. I say this because from the time I walked into that office, I felt as though they were not very helpful. I sat in the lobby for a while before I received any help. Altogether, the whole appointment was not positive. When it was time to show me around the complex, I was only shown one model apartment and for me, that it not enough. To be honest, I cannot believe I was so disappointed about something so small. I guess it stems from being in college and sharing a dorm room and apartment for years. I have always liked the idea of being able to decorate a space and call it my own. I will keep that hope alive and one day that dream will come true.

Now it is time for me to focus on the gift I have. Speaking of gifts, I always get confused about whether God only blessed me with just one. I think this way because I have accomplished so much in track. I know deep down, God put me here to minister to young females because I have a strong story to tell and I am not ashamed of it. I know that God has a purpose for my life. I am learning that because I have experienced a lot at a young age, the Lord can use me in many ways. Whatever the Lord chooses to do, I am going to be grateful. In this season, I knew it was going to be hard, but not this hard. I just pray that something works out.

I need a local sponsor or something. Gosh, these workouts are hard. I remember when I thought I would not be able to run anything over two hundred meters, let alone a single five hundred. I just want to be happy, run fast, and be a role model. *Lord, I thank You for changing my heart. Sometimes I feel like my heart is broken forever. But even in times of despair, I can smile. I just wish things were different, not easy, but just different. Lord, I need You, I need You now. I realize I cannot do it without You.* I have no choice, but to push through. With only .91 cent in my bank account, giving up is not an option. I want people to hear my story and know the struggle that comes with being a professional athlete. I know it sounds like a bunch of rambling, but if this is what I must do to chase my dreams, then this is it. I never wanted to chase this dream for self-gratification; I am doing it because I feel like it is my calling. Moreover, some of my closest friends have become distant, but maybe that is because we chose a different route in life. With having so many trials in life, I have learned to be my own cheerleader. You cannot look for people to applaud you because people change.

The 9 to 5

Romans 8:18 "I consider that our present sufferings are not worth comparing with the glory that will be revealed in us."

The 9 to 5 is temporary, and I already know

Feels like a boat and I am sinking, but I must keep rowing

The Word says don't get weary in doing what's good

But often I feel alone and misunderstood

I try to do what is right in my Father's eyes

But God I know You hear me praying on this 1-hour drive

You gave me a promise

I see it plain as day

You are the potter, I am the clay

You know my heart, You know my thoughts, I just want to give back

I knew that I would make it, but wow not in track

You said in "due season"

Well I am looking for next summer

I can tell you about my life and how it keeps me humble.

I wrote this short poem while working my most recent 9 to 5 job. I am no stranger to hard work seeing how I have worked since the age of 16. I know that I must do whatever is necessary to live the life I have dreamed. At my last desk job, which ended on October 26th, I felt a change of heart after I received my personalized desk plaque with my name written in bold letters. I immediately took a permanent marker out of the desk drawer and wrote on the back "this is my last desk job." I say all of that to say this, I know that I was chosen by God to do something different, something big. I will not settle.

On the other hand, I have met so many inspirational people who have touched my heart in ways you could never imagine. Whether it was working in a warehouse, customer service, a shoe store, or a grocery delivery company, I met some amazing people. I encourage you to take time out of your work schedule to really look around and see how blessed you are. Someone is always doing worse than you. If you were like me, a professional athlete working full-time during the offseason to somewhat sponsor yourself for the upcoming season, just know that it is temporary. The early morning and long nights cannot be compared to the goals we are going to achieve.

The Therapist from Heaven

On August 12, 2015, I made my first appointment to see a therapist. It is a dark, gloomy night and I can hear the voices telling me I have not let go of my past. I am still the same person I was in high school. It is unbearable, too much for me to handle. I find myself in the closet, on my knees, with my face planted on the light brown carpet. It was my hiding place, the one thing I was afraid of, the dark. Ms. Moyer said I should try to find a therapist, but I have no idea how to go about doing that, she told me to call my insurance company. Whatever, I guess I will give it another try, why not? I tried a while back but got discouraged because there were so many to choose from. I did not know which direction to go in. Not only that, but I told a few people about my concerns, and they were not here for it. Most people thought I was exaggerating about my problems. I grab my insurance card from my wallet, I called the number on the back, and before they could recite their opening statement, I cut the representative off and said, "I am not okay, and I need help." She paused, and I could hear her whisper, "Go get the supervisor on this call, NOW." I could not believe the words that were coming out of my mouth. The supervisor was on the call now, and she asked for my address, so they could baker act me. A fancy way of saying, we are going to put you in custody involuntarily until we know that you are okay to go home and not have those self-defeating thoughts. After talking for about thirty minutes, I assured them that I was okay.

Five minutes later, my brother walks in. I kept it to myself and walked into my room and closed the door. I was used to that, hiding my feelings, being strong and saying that everything was okay when it really was not. I woke up the next morning and told him I was going to seek professional help, and he said I should go if that is what I think will help me. Although we were raised in different households, my brother always understood what I was going through, and he was very supportive. I knew I had to work a full shift that day, so I intended to find a faith-based counselor I could speak to. For some reason, I felt as though they would be more transparent and honest with me.

Growing up, it was frowned upon to see a counselor because

people in my community did not believe in such things. I knew I had to do this for myself. It was too much to keep inside. I was a volcano waiting to erupt. After hours of searching local offices and having short phone interviews, I found one! Although I mentioned it to my brother, I did not tell anyone I decided to go. I had to do this for me. I walked in, met the therapist and before I realized it, I was already judging her by how young she looked. I thought to myself, she probably has not been through as much as I have, and she gets paid for this, but I was willing to give her a chance. At this point, I had nothing to lose but a lot to gain.

I sat in her office; it was not like the places you see on television. The walls were not white, and she was not wearing a fancy doctor's coat. She had on regular clothes, and her office was warm with a glass dish full of candy on the side. It reminded me of the old times I sat in Ms. Moyer's office in high school. My exact words were this, "I think I am crazy." She laughs and says, "You are not crazy, you are twenty-four, and you have experienced a lot. You have been trying to process everything on your own, but you are not crazy." Then she proceeds to say that most crazy people do not know they are crazy. I guess she had a valid point there. She said I was doing a great job at everything, but she will help me dissect what happened so that way I could move forward.

For the first time in a long time, I met someone who was completely unbiased and was open to whatever I had to say. I did not mention anything about being a professional runner; I wanted her to get to know me, the real Alexis Love. She let me talk and cry, and then talk and cry some more. A cry I had waited so long to let out. It was not like those hard cries I would have in the shower every week, but it was a sigh of relief. I felt my soul being set free. I had peace like never before. I could see things more clearly. I could process and comprehend things I had never understood before. We started out with introducing little Alexis, baby girl, the four-year-old that was always crying for help. Although this is twenty years later, little Alexis felt like someone was listening to her. She was being redeemed and set free. In that very moment, I had forgiven the people who hurt me in my past, but I wanted closure. I know now that it all had to start with me. I had to be willing and open to set myself free. The truth hurts, but the truth will also set you free. Forgiveness is not easy, but again it is necessary and could be the one thing that is blocking your blessings.

Part III: Victory is Yours

Personal Diary Entries

Today is the big day, November 11, 2015! In three hours or less, I will be a new creation, and everything I did in the past will not matter. I am going to feel and act brand new. *Thank You, Jesus, for saving me. I do not deserve what You did for me, but I am forever grateful.* I have waited for this day my whole life. Well, ten years to be exact so I guess that is a long time. I am so happy!! I finally have peace after all those years. People are saying they see the change in me and that I am glowing. I keep telling them, it is not me, but God who changed me. From the inside out, He made me new. Now I am ready to publicly identify that I have accepted Christ as my Savior. I am not saying I am perfect, but I am striving to be more like Christ. Why not start now and do things the right way? Like most new Christians in their walk, I thought you had to be perfect to get baptized, and once you are baptized then you have a ticket to Heaven, boy was I confused. Now I know why the other baptism dates I set in Texas did not work out.

On my way to get baptized a year ago, I was stuck in traffic, and the other time I arrived on the wrong date. I am so sure God knew I needed to do more research and gain a full understanding of the meaning of baptism before I was submerged in the water. So now that I am back home, feeling brand new and refreshed, I am ready to post that one picture for the people who missed it. The peace I have now is one I cannot describe with words. I was a little nervous when they put the spotlight on the warm pool of water, but I was ready. I made a commitment that this is one race I will run forever if I have God on my side. Angela and Fabian were there in the audience to support me, and I was thankful for that. Gosh, I was so emotional. Angela is my sister on my dad's side. She is also the twin to my brother, AJ, who I was living with at the time. Fabian is her boyfriend. What a wonderful feeling that I will never forget. That very thing was just right for me, even the temperature and small bubbles in the water. I know this beginning will also bring new challenges. It is imperative that I renew my mind daily. I know I will also have to let go of old things and habits to receive new things in my life.

The Other Side

Work for it, there is no substitute for hard work.

"Faith without works is dead." I used to read this verse over and over. I assumed that because I was a new creation in Christ that things would just fall out of the sky. In a way, I felt as though I was entitled to my blessings, but the one ingredient I was missing was the one thing that held me back. I completely missed the part where it says, 'without works.' I believed without a doubt that I was going to be successful. However, I forgot to work for it. I spent hours training, preparing my physical and spiritual muscles, but when it was time to perform, I left my weapons behind. I came to the battle with no armor. Who shows up to a war without a sword? Yea, that was me. I learned that even though you have matured in reading books, you still need help at times in seeing the unseen and understanding on a different level. It has been said that I tend to overthink things, but in all actuality, overthinking helps me digest what it is I am trying to comprehend. I am sure I am not the only one. Have you ever read a passage then ten minutes later you cannot remember what you just read? Knowledge is power, but what good is having power if we do not know how to use it? You must be confident in what you know and do not let anyone change that.

There is no substitute for hard work. I have not found any routine or ritual that will accelerate you to the next level. I remember my high school athletic director, Coach Woodie said, "Alexis you can be a big fish in a small sea." He was not saying you will make it for sure, but I believe he was saying it may be hard, other fish may get in the way, but if you work hard and keep swimming, you can become a big fish.

Tips with love: Friends, whether your sea is big or small, whether you are a whale or a goldfish, you can eat, and you can get to the top. Again, you are only a prisoner to the cage you allow yourself to be trapped in. Sometimes that cage is your mind. You cannot do what you cannot see, and you cannot be what you cannot believe. Believe it, live it, and act on it. I can truly say that hard work does pay off. I knew that if I continued to persevere and work hard that the door of opportunity would eventually open for me.

She Had a Dream

I spoke with my dad one bright and sunny afternoon, and I shared with him that I had a dream. The dream was as real as they got. I was running the 200-meter dash in a big race, and the crowd was cheering, but I could not hear anything. The same level of focus I had during my first track meet was the same focus I had in my dream. The gun went off, and I came around the curve, blazing fast with an extra set of wings, no arms just wings. Swinging them back and forth, I was ahead of the pack. Next thing you know, the commentator is on the loudspeaker announcing, "Alexis Love, 200m champion!" The crowd goes crazy, and I fall to my knees, weeping on the track, I could not move. That moment seemed like it lasted a lifetime. Before I could enjoy the last few moments, I was awakened by the sound of a voice, "Alexis are you going to work today?"

To be honest, I wanted to live The American Dream. Oh, the sweet sound of democracy, rights, liberty, opportunity, and equality. Where freedom includes the opportunity for prosperity and success as well as an upward social mobility for the family and children, achieved through hard work in a society with few barriers. If you were to search the Internet for what it means to live The American Dream, I am sure you would find a similar definition. Furthermore, I have looked at my own life and concluded that I am living out my very own dream. It was created by not being afraid to take risks, believing in myself, hard work, and sacrifice. One of the most important things I have learned is at times you must be your own sponsor before you have an official sponsor who is looking to invest in you. Do not get discouraged, all great things take time. While it may sound like I have it all figured out at such a young age, I am still learning and evolving. I was once told, if you find out what does not work for you, then you are halfway to discovering what does work.

Victory Awaits at the Finish Line

Tips with love: You need to know that you are a winner before you even start the race. I am referring to the race of life in this sense. Everything you have gone through or experienced up to this point has prepared you for this very moment. Everything looks familiar because you have been here before. This is not a debate about whether I believe in Déjà Vu, but I am simply putting it this way, if it looks and sounds familiar, then this is your opportunity to respond differently this time around. Life lessons are here to help you grow, but often we do not want to grow through the process. I wish I had learned this concept at a younger age, but hey, timing is everything. Everyone likes to wish they could turn back the hands of time, but your brain cannot accept what your age has not dealt with internally, in the heart. A universal theme is that, If I can look great on the outside, then I can cover up what is going on inside. This is dangerous. I lived that lie for way too long. MAC, Clinique, whatever you choose-- nothing can hide the hurt of pain and abuse. We tend to cover our faces instead of facing the issue. You are more than a conqueror. You have already won the victory. You are a goal medal winner before you receive the medal in your hand. You are unstoppable. You cannot be defeated. Look up and smile, beloved, victory waits at the finish line. After all, who can take what is already yours?

God, thank You for making me the strong woman I am today. Thank You for helping me discover my identity in Christ. I am not perfect, but I strive to live for You and You only. You changed my inward beauty, so it will reflect my beauty on the outside. I love You so much, and I want to continue to walk closely with You.

Anything Is Possible

Tips with love: It is true, we can do whatever we put our minds to. It is never too late to live out your childhood dreams. Anything is possible when you realize that what you need is already inside of you. There comes a time in life where you stop searching for the answers and hidden secrets and realize that there is no secret to success. Having like-minded people around is a key factor to the puzzle. I believe there is no way possible to fail when your mind is made up. In the past, I have second guessed myself about what it is I can do, and it all makes sense now. If your vision is not clear, how are you able to see the path to get there? You must know without a doubt that you were put on this earth to be amazing, to do the unthinkable, and to be extraordinary. I always knew there was something different about me, and while for some people different may be confusing at first. I have come to terms that I was made to stand out. I am the chosen one, and it had to be me. No one can do what I was called to do both on and off the track. You need to make a short list compiled of five things that will keep you going when you feel down in a slump. Growing up, I have always admired the celebrities from my hometown and wanted to be like them. Fast forward, now that I can be that person in my community, I would not have it any other way. I want to give those kids hope. I have realized that my past enables me to help others. It does not disqualify me.

Things that keep me going when life wants to knock me down:

1) I have come too far, and I have worked too hard

2) The people are counting on me

3) I want to prove the naysayers wrong

4) I made a promise to Little Alexis

5) The pain I endured pushes me. I must win

What is your why? List them below:

1)

2)

3)

4)

5)

He knows my name. I know my life changed when I began to smile again. I knew it was real when I found my true friend. His name is Jesus. He made me feel what I have never felt before, unconditional love. A love that could only come from above. At that point, I wanted to live for him. Our father is really in heaven, and I have no doubt about that. His Word is all truths, nothing, but facts. Once I started believing again, I started achieving. Achieving my goals in life, becoming a better person. I could love again. I was on the path to see myself the way He did. He loves you too, and I want you to know that! But first, you must close that door. You must die to yourself and seek him with your whole heart. I trusted Him with everything in me, and he showed me who He wanted me to be. I love Him so much that words cannot express. I never thought in a million years I could be so blessed. I remember when I wanted to sin, I remember having a lot of friends; I remember mostly everything from way back then. It caused me so much hurt and pain. Now I know how to forgive, I know how to repent. I know right from wrong and what is heaven sent. I know that I am beautiful; I know that I am smart, and I just want you to know that you can have this too, but first, you must start.

Resilience

Father, I want to do what You saw me doing before I was in my mother's womb. I want Your will to be done, not mine. I want the dream You put in my heart to come to pass. I believe in You wholeheartedly. I believe You have great things in store for me. This whole time I did not understand it, but now I know for sure that You have a plan and purpose for my life. Thank You for taking me on the long and scenic route to my destiny. Thank You for preparing me for the blessing. Thank You for the good and the bad days, they have made me strong and taught me how to persevere. When I turned this page in this specific journal, you confirmed that this is a new chapter, a new beginning for me. You have sent me so many confirmations in Your Word through several people, and now I receive it and believe it. Thank You for all the restless nights when you revealed things to me. Thank You for sending Angels to confirm a vision you have placed inside me. I see it now. I am ready for what is to come. I am doing this for You. In 2012, You saved my soul and loved me like no other. You forgave me repeatedly. You chose me. You called me out. You qualified me, you promoted me. You have declared that it shall happen. Lord, forgive me for taking this long to trust in You and Your word. Your word is true, it gives me life. Without You I am nothing, and I know I cannot do this on my own. Thank You for making me the head and not the tail. Thank You for making me more than a conqueror. Thank You for making me a victor and turning my pain into my strength. You have kept me here for a reason. Thank you for setting me free. I can never thank You enough for changing my life. You saw the best in me. You knew every thought and feeling I had since my childhood days when I was a little girl. After all this time, Little Alexis finally has closure and peace. I feel so much lighter. You broke every chain, and now it is time for me to rise in victory! I could not have made it this far without You. You wrapped your loving arms around me when no one else would. You protected me and kept me throughout the years. It was Your grace and mercy. It all makes sense now. You allowed me to go through things because you knew I would come out solid, stronger than I have ever been before.

So here it is, the time is now. I am ready to walk into my destiny with You. I am ready to soar with my new wings. I am ready to live out my dream and fulfill the purpose and calling You have over my life. I am ready to be a light to the world. I want to make Your name great and glorify You on this stage at the trials. You created me in your image, lacking nothing. I have confidence in You and Your word. I believe it will come to pass. Father, thank you in advance for making me number one, thank you for making me an Olympian. Thank you for blessing me in front of my enemies. Thank you for Your supernatural strength, power, and speed. Thank you for empowering me to be the fastest woman in the world. Thank you for the special time and place You have set aside to bless me. Most of all, thank you for choosing me even when I am undeserving. I will always come back to say, thank you. I am on your wheel, you are the potter, mold me and shape me into what You want me to be and do at the trials. This is more than the Olympic Trials; this is a trial I cannot see in the natural. Help me, Lord.

Olympic Trials and Life Trials

My dad said this, "Negativity should be a stepping stone that you can learn and grow from. From this point on, you must run and not look back. You must remain focused on what is ahead of you. You grow every day, but only if you choose to do so." From the time I was a little girl, my dad always knew what to say. In a sense, he reminded me of how Jesus used parables to speak to the people. I am now seeing a different side of my dad. I had the urge to shout, dad just spit it out, but he always got the point across and that is what matters.

Looking back, I would like to think that everything I have gone through so far was preparing me for womanhood. Now I am here, I have arrived. More resilient than ever, I am ready to make my dreams a reality. No more wishing, no more guessing, but natural talent, hard work, and a drive like none other.

Tip with love: To be resilient, you must get out of your own way. You must reach beyond the stars and push yourself to the limit. You must know that being your own number one fan is vital to your success. At times, you may want to quit, the dream may seem impossible, but if it were easy everyone would do it. To me, hearing the words, only the strong survive, is an incomplete statement. You will, and you can survive whatever it is that life throws at you, but surviving is just the beginning. I believe we are not put on this earth to only survive by worldly standards, but we are here to thrive, to do the unthinkable. One day at a time you will gain a new supporter/fan, a new friend, and a new strength.

God says He is a lamp to our path. This is an important reminder for me because I am curious about what is going to happen next month or next year and I forget to focus on tomorrow. Running in the Olympics while representing Team USA is the goal for most runners in Track and Field. The Olympics is the one place in the world where you get to see the best compete against each other. Although I have run in two U.S. Olympic Trials, it is different from the actual Olympics. However, I believe that I am one of the best to ever do it. If you think about it, almost everyone who is at the top of their game thinks they too are the best. A person may or may not admit it, but to achieve a certain level of success, you must believe that you are great, and you have all the tools to become an expert in your field. In the good book, all the runners run, but you must run in the way that you will receive the prize.

Trust me, I do not recall anyone asking me if I wanted to stand next to them on the podium to share their first-place title. I also do not recall anyone asking me if I would like to take their lane or place on the track. I say that to say this, if you want it you must go get it. Nothing is going to be handed to you, and if you are like me, I chose the hard route. In all honesty, the tougher route chose me and because life dealt me this specific hand of cards, I must play them. In a card game, you cannot control what cards you are dealt, but you can play them to the best of your ability. People can scream and yell over your shoulder as if they know which cards you need to play, but at the end of the day, you must follow your gut and do what is best.

Life itself taught me how to be resilient. When I stumbled upon what it meant to be resilient, I learned that it is the capacity to recover quickly from difficulties and/or toughness. Another definition describes resilience as the ability of an object to spring back into shape. I cannot help but to compare myself to this definition. What I have gone through in life, was not meant to keep me out of shape for forever, but to bend me temporarily. When it was time to snap back into shape and recover, I did it quickly. That, my friends, is what you call resilience. I am by no means arrogant or feel as if I made it this far on my own, but I think it is the time that I give myself credit for having the willingness to recover from such tragedies and difficulties in life. Everyone is not willing to take the road less traveled, but after being on this path, I discovered that I was made for it. I was created for greatness. My story was already written, even at the age of four. Who knew a life to love would be birthed from so much pain and anger? Who knew that little girl would be used and most importantly, who knew that girl would blossom into a beautiful woman who would someday change lives?

Concerning the Olympics and life, we all have our very own personal race to run. No one can run it for us, and no one is called to do it but us. In this race of life, we must prepare ourselves for what is ahead, stay in our lane, and stop at nothing. There was one common theme I found in all my coaches throughout the years, they stressed the importance of running through the finish line. Some people lean too early and cause others to run pass them to get what was theirs. I understand the importance of leaning because, at times, the race comes down to the ten-thousandth of a second, but then, there are others who have been sent out on a mission to get the victory which is already theirs. Through hard work, faith, and determination they have found their inner strength. They do not wait for others to validate their level of greatness; they already know they are great. They lace-up their spikes, show up to the check-in tents, and they are ready to go. Not focused on anyone else, but themselves and the finish line, they soar through the finish line with wings like eagles. They run and do not get weary, and they press toward to the goal to win for which God has called them.

I am here to let you know, it is possible. The dreams and

visions you have in the middle of the day or late at night are real. I know because I had many dreams and I still do. I was told that I live my life as if it was a fairytale, but I do not get offended. I took that statement as a compliment. If you ask me, some fairytales have a happy ending, why not choose happiness after experiencing hurt and sorrow for years? Like a fairytale, why not hope and wish for the best? Why not be different and do something remarkable in life that has others saying, "Wow, she is living a fairytale!" I believe it is no different than the American Dream. Growing up, I believed there was only one American Dream, but I forced myself to look at that differently. You can have your own dream, it does not have to be made up of accomplishments set by worldly standards, like me, it can be the peace and satisfaction in knowing that years later, you are doing the very thing you said you were going to do as a child.

Dreams do not have to end once you get older, I am teaching myself to never stop dreaming and never stop believing. It is never too late to have an okay childhood. Sometimes when you are at the end of your ropes that is the beginning of a new start. Sacrifice is doing what is necessary to be the best version of yourself. Whether it be moving fourteen hours away to attend a university in Murray, Kentucky or leaving behind everything you once knew to fulfill a dream that no one has seen, but you. Nevertheless, I persevered and made it. Not seeing a way out but making a way out. If you had told me I was going to sacrifice and make so many life decisions, I would have bailed out before I signed my official letter to turn professional in the sport of track and field. Hard work and sacrifice have become familiar to me these days. I am in no way complaining or wishing things were easier.

However, I am simply stating this, ready or not, life will throw curve balls, but what matters is how you respond. Will you fight back or become numb to the situation? Life itself has taught me how to be strong when I thought I could not go on. Besides growing my faith, being stronger both mentally and physically, track has also taught me, sacrifice. I speak so much of this one word because this is basically what it comes down to. What are you willing to give up to accomplish your lifelong dreams and goals?

Tips with love: I used to be concerned with being able to bring everyone on my journey to the Olympics but soon realized, no one can run the race, but me. There will be times where you must leave some people behind, but please know this is vital to your success. If you have ever heard the famous words, 'love them from a distance,' well, this is one of those times. Now fast forward, this is where I am today; happy, full of joy, and living a life that I love!

As it relates to track, I used to get frustrated at times and wanted things to happen overnight. One of my training partners would say, "You know Rome was not built in a day." I thought it was a trick to get me to overthink something once again, but now that I look back, I realize, it is what it is. It was the truth, and the truth is what I needed. No more questioning if someone had ill intentions for me because I was beyond that, but just taking things for what they are. The seasons go by in track and field, and the more I become a student at the sport, the more I learn. I am learning that if you want to be great, you must do whatever it takes. Even if you are working on your dream, day in and day out, it still takes time. Some of the greatest athletes I have admired have a story about their journey and the time it took to get there. My mentor, Pat Williams said it best, "Preparation breeds confidence." If I am confident in what I am doing, then I am already on the road to being great. Being great takes time, and I am willing to do it.

Some people get to the finish line and are afraid of what is on the other side, or they stop too early, not knowing that victory is not far off. In this sport, you are not respected when you are not running fast. Simple things like trying to chime in on a conversation is not welcomed when you are not one of the favorites. I am not asking for sympathy, but I am noticing certain changes that I must make. Get this, it is no one else's responsibility, but my own to make sure I am relevant. I am the only one who can change that. As stated earlier, all great things take time.

The Outcome

After the 2016 U.S., Olympic Trials, my second attempt, I was done mentally. I was drained, and my mind was made up about working a "regular" job. Not even days after arriving back to Florida after the Olympic trials, I decided to wake up the next Saturday morning to cut my hair off again. I figured if I could cut out the old part of me then the new me would come alive.

Get this, friends, man looks at the outward appearance, and God looks at the heart. At this point, I was spiritually depleted and could not go on. No one could ever go on and try to accomplish something so big on their own. Without strength from a higher power, how will we ever reach our destination? Looking back over my life, I realized God had His hand on my life the whole time.

I can try my best to protect myself from suffering again, but then again, it is not my job. The outcome will be what it is going to be. One may argue that we are in total control while others think the outcome was written before we were born. Spiritual or not, you will one day realize that you can only control what is going on in this moment and focus on the present. I have missed so many wonderful things by focusing on the future. Being consumed with the outcome will have you going through your day with the notion that things will never change. You start to do a routine and life gets dull.

Ponder this, what if life was ready for you, but you were never ready for life? This reminds me of the famous quote by Dr. Martin Luther King Jr., "Faith is taking the first step even when you don't see the whole staircase." I was focused seeing the top of the staircase that I forgot to enjoy the journey. Knowing that I will someday reach the top, gave me peace and joy. It is something I no longer had to think about. Trust me, it was not easy, but it was worth it. The ups and downs, the challenges, the victories, it was all worth it. When I say, I came from the bottom, I am not necessarily saying that I struggled growing up, but what I am saying is that life was a struggle at times. One of my biggest fears in life was not being successful. The thought alone was enough to change my attitude after middle school. I was getting in trouble, had Saturday school and detention, but I decided to do something different. It was not pleasant, but I knew there was a greater reward in the end. Besides, I promised 'Little Alexis she would someday have peace and be set free. I like to sit and think it was all an illusion, but no, these things really happened. I am in no way ashamed of my past because without my journal entries, tears and dark moments, I would have never considered the thought of having a life to love. A life to love is finding peace and joy right where you are. It is about knowing you have a friend that sticks closer than a brother when everyone has left you. It is about being your own cheerleader when you feel as though the world has turned its back on you, and most importantly, it is knowing that someday, you will look back and say it was all worth it. I believe we all have a story, but my question to you is this, what is keeping you from sharing your story? I am sure you know by now the thoughts and opinions of others are merely just that, but what matters is what you think of yourself. If you think you can, then you will.

Disappoint them or fulfill my destiny? If I have not learned anything else in this world, one thing I know for sure is that everyone will not support you on your journey. In fact, most people will not understand the vision God has for you. It took me a long time to understand that. The same people that told me not to cut my hair after the 2016 Olympic Trials are the same people telling me this haircut fits my 'track runner look.' One minute the world will support you, and the next they are nowhere to be found. I would rather disappoint others if that is what it takes to fulfill my destiny. I have always told myself the best is yet to come. If this is true, then what I want to accomplish in the world will be much greater than becoming the fastest woman in the world.

Tip with love: If not you, then who? Of course, many people have done it before you and others will do it after you, but no one can do it like you.

Today, as I take a moment to reflect, I ask myself, why did I care about other's feelings so much more than my own. People are funny. They will tell you that it is not the right time and your goals are too farfetched and perhaps you should start small. I beg to differ. Time waits for no man or woman. Some things and people are meant to be left behind to fulfill your destiny.

Only You Can Tell Your Story

They say it is easy to let go, but I beg to differ. Part of me wants to move on, but I fear the new me. The new me is good and everything I prayed for, but sometimes it is shocking, and it is hard to accept the fact that He paid for it.

My new life is something that I did not earn, but by His stripes, I am healed, and that is my only concern. I want to live right and do His will, but then there is that deep thought that tells me to chill. My purpose is to help others by sharing my story. I wonder why it is so hard for others to give Him the glory. I know it sounds like a bunch of rhymes and you consider it boring, but who am I to act like I did not go through life worrying. Of course, this is contrary to what the world wants to see, but if not me then who will it be?

I wrote this entry after being criticized for sharing my story. I always say, be careful when you pray and ask God to use you in a mighty way because you may not be ready; well at least I wasn't. My story is part of my testimony, and I know my testimony is part of my mission. Sharing my story was not so much about justifying my past, but it was about courage. Courage to share the truth in the face of opposition. My mission is to help others by sharing my life experiences. It seems like people are living in the dark, not because they want to, but because they are afraid of the new person. 1 John: 6-7 says, "If we say we have fellowship with him and yet keep on walking in the darkness, we are lying and not practicing the truth."

Choosing to walk with God was one of the hardest things I had ever done, but it was also the most important decision I had ever made. The truth will set you free, but the truth also hurts. I was able to start healing once I faced the truth and decided to stop running from it. I moved to a different state, I changed my number, I ran for miles and miles, and it all came back to the one thing I did not want to face. It is a choice to want to live right and a choice to share your story. If I had to do it all over again, it would have never been an option. What if you could live a better life? What if everything was to work in your favor? The time is now. You can live a better life.

A Family That Prays -1 John 4:7-11 says "Beloved, let us love one another, for love is from God, and whoever loves has been born of God and know God. Anyone who does not love does not know God because God is love..." To know that Jesus loved me before I loved myself is all the confidence I need to love others. God hates the sins we commit, but He still loves us. Some may argue that love is more than a word, it is also an action. Real love is loving someone beyond their faults and flaws. Love never fails. I am speaking of love as it is relevant to relationships. To love your family, spouses, business, brand, etc., you must love God first. Loving God more than you love the person or thing is what matters in the end. Knowing these things, you will understand the true meaning of His word when He says, "Love never fails." We only have our families and friends here on earth for such a short time. That is what led me to practice agape love. This is the type of love that will cause you to do good regardless of your feelings and emotions. It is unconditional love. Loving beyond life's conditions. I am very passionate when it comes to my family and I treasure them all. Family is not always blood, but by the blood, we can become family. I have met people on my journey who have treated me as if they have known me from birth. That is true love, building each other up. I have prayed for a family that would love on each other and be supportive no matter what. Who can tear down a family that prays? No one. That bond is unbreakable.

Soon, I will show my family just how much I love them. I have a speaking engagement and the topic is near to my heart. God has been preparing me for this moment my whole life. He has molded me and shaped me into the woman I am today. He has used so many things to teach and guide me in the way He wants me to go. He has taught me how to persevere through trials and hard times. I have learned how to keep the faith. I am ready to deliver this speech and change lives. As I sat in the car parked outside the church, I could hardly keep my composure. I was so ecstatic about speaking at a local church in my hometown and sharing my story. The title of the conference was, 'You don't know my story.' What I thought was a good idea was not so good. I thought it was the perfect set-up to have me speak at a women's conference, especially with that title. I prepared for the engagement days ahead. Instead of using a notecard, the Lord allowed me to speak from the heart. As I began to share my story, I could see everyone in the audience with the same look on their face. They had the look of confusion as if they could not believe I was still standing after all I had gone through. I went on to end my speech and shortly after returning to my seat, I received a bunch of text messages. Some of the messages were encouraging, and others were not so nice. Some were upset at the fact that I was telling the secret and others thought I was disrespecting my family. However, that was never my intention. I only wanted to share my struggles to help the next woman, man or teenager. It is a very hurtful thing when you think you are doing the right thing, but then feel disowned for doing it. Rejection tries to creep in, but I will not allow that in my life.

The next morning, I woke up with puffy eyes from the restless night before. I looked as if I had not slept in days. I was weeping. I thought it was what my family wanted. The truth shall set you free, right? Whom the son sets free, he is free indeed. The truth is the truth, right?

There was a lot revealed in one night, one night of endless tears. I know the Lord was with me. He even sent my earthly father to sit in the audience, so I would have someone physically there. I am so glad my friend Kiara was in attendance as well, Lord knows I cried on her shoulder for a while. I really needed that. I tried so hard not to cry in front of my dad because I know he just wants to see his baby girl happy. I guess the next time around I should not share the details. I have one more speaking engagement at my home church then after that I am shutting it down and focusing solely on my own personal goals. I am going to pray on this because I know the enemy wants to keep me silent. I know the Lord wants me to speak out. He made me bold and courageous. I have wanted to give everyone peace for so long, I feel like I owe it to them. Not the case, some people want to be trapped--something I will never understand. I can only rescue and speak life into those who are receptive to it.

Lord, I asked You to use me, and You did, in a mighty way, I must add. Lord, You also showed me that I cannot go back for everyone. You know the tears I cried. I wish I could just sit on the clouds and tell You all about it face to face. I find it funny my dad said he had no idea why he was there, but he knew it was a reason. Lord, it was You sitting next to me, wrapping Your arms around me to let me know I was not alone. Everything will be alright. I tried to write notes, but You wanted me to speak from the spirit. Forgive me if I have done wrong. I was only speaking from a place of love. Through it all, on this day You gave me the strength to go on. Now that everyone is watching and listening. Now that You have grabbed their attention, I will continue to speak up. I can literally see my family being transformed one day.

Maybe it will take 5, 10, or 20 years, but now is the time to plant seeds. I will never understand why you chose me, but I am grateful. I cannot put it off any longer. I have no time to waste to do the Lord's work. I must do this. I surrender my dreams, gifts, and everything to you, Lord. I only want to please you. You were there when no one else was.

Temporary Distractions

Why do we get focused only to allow a distraction to throw us off course? For example, we know that we were put on this earth for a specific purpose. We can have our minds made up and know just how detrimental a distraction can be, but we allow them to creep in. How focused are you? If you were that focused, you would not give your precious time away in the first place. Before I go on, let me clear the air and say this, I am not saying you should be so focused that you forget to enjoy the beauty of life. I am saying, there is a fine line between being successful and not being successful. It is all about how you utilize your time. If you are one who has mastered the balance of time in your personal and work life, then go for it. So please keep this in mind, temporary distractions can come from almost anywhere if you allow it to. The key is to know what grabs your attention to the point where you are no longer able to focus. Keep your eyes fixed on what matters, the goal. Regarding your followers and worrying about time spent on social media to gain social status, just relax. God will send the followers when perhaps you start following Him. This is not a forceful statement; this is what I have experienced in my personal life. Time is on your side if you utilize it correctly.

Concerning temporary distractions, I must be honest and own up to my mistakes first. During my Fall Training in the years 2015 and 2016, I let everything stress me out. I was worried about doing everything perfect and concerned with what others thought of me. I was not focused. I believed the lies about myself that I know did not come from the Lord. I believed I was overweight and needed to starve myself to get into shape. Come to find out, I only needed guidance in nutrition as it relates to my sport. At the end of the day, all I had to do was just run. There were times that I felt like the world was on my shoulders and I was suffocating. As Dr. Paul, would say, "I need to focus on what I can control, so when the call comes, I will not be caught off guard." He always gives good advice when I need it. So yeah, I accept full responsibility for not being where I want to be at this point in my life. I should be more kind to myself.

While most of you may think, I have it all it together, I am nowhere near perfect. I have caused many blessings to be delayed. Like Joshua in the Bible, the land was already mine, I need only to take possession of it. I promise I will never get distracted again. I put it this way, God knows the desires of our hearts and so does the enemy. He can dress them up, make them put on your favorite fragrance and do whatever it takes to get you off course. Friends be strong! Use that spirit of discernment you have or just plain common sense. I long for a relationship, but if I am honest, I am not ready for a relationship. I am not ready to date, and I need to keep my focus on Him because even the right guy at the wrong time is the wrong guy, if that makes any sense. I do get lonely at times, but I know the Lord will send a godly man when He is ready... I am not trying to rush at all.

Social media versus being real. For most people, it is all about the thrill. It is almost like their life is so perfect., but 1,000 likes later you wonder if it was worth it.

I was inclined to write this short message after spending too much time on social media. How do I know when it is too much time? When my priorities are out of place, i.e., scrolling on social media when I have work to do. Another indicator is when I wake up in the morning, and the first thing I do is check Instagram, Facebook, and now Snapchat. That is when you know it is entirely too much. To be honest, just this past week I decided to do a one week fast from it all. The benefits are life-changing. I am not saying this to exaggerate, but seriously it works. For example, I could focus more on the task at hand, I woke up well-rested because I went to bed on time, I had free time, and I could fill that time with growing spiritually. Without being aware of this issue I was making these things my god, so to speak. Checking notifications before checking in with God. So now I have decided to delete the apps from my iPhone and put them on my iPad. I know this will work because my iPad is always dead for the most part and I do not carry it with me. I am not saying social media is bad because it is a great tool for networking but can also be a distraction.

I have a different outlook on time as it relates to my life purpose. Time is valuable. It is something you can never get back. For me personally, time is something I cannot afford to waste. I understand that I may not have time to change the entire world, but I can change the world with the time I do have. It is all about how you plan your day.

It Was Not Easy

If I do not share anything else, I must share this; Life is a journey, and it is important that you enjoy every moment. While everyone has their own battles they are facing, I believe most people find hope in reading someone else's story about how they came out victorious. In certain cases, that is what it is, a battle in the mind. We must win in our minds first. That is one of the principles I live by. During a tough time, we may think that no one else has experienced what we are going through, but keep in mind, you will not be the first or last to encounter a struggle. What has helped me in the past is searching for people who have experienced some of the same heartaches I had and hearing their success stories. After all, everyone loves a victory, a win, or a happy ending. If you search for it, you will find it. There is no secret to success. It is about mastering the little things and doing them consistently. It is about living in a positive light. As it relates to track and field, it is not about what song you listen to before the race or wearing your favorite socks or bracelet on competition day. I have realized you do not need the gold spikes to win gold. There is no substitute for hard work. Never second guess yourself because of your past. If you put in the work, you will always get results.

I am blessed. The more I meditate on that, the more I believe it. God is still good. *Dear God, create in me a clean heart, place the right people in my life. Open the door that only you can open.* I cannot believe I am sitting outside in the dark trying to journal. I must admit, it is kind of hard to put pressure on myself and go hard every day when all I have experienced is the struggle. I must make it out. I believe that God is a promise keeper and He stays true to his word. I know He has not forgotten about me. The dream I had when I was a little girl will come to pass. I feel as though I am beginning to walk into my destiny.

Come to think of it, Ms. Moyer says I was always in survival mode ever since I was a child. She goes on to say that I was always fighting. I felt like I was not, but then again that was me being in denial about my past. Deep down, I agree with Ms. Moyer. After all, she is the one I ran to every day for four years during my high school career. The way she loved and cared for me is still a mystery to me. She advised me to also do research on kids coming from some sort of poverty because that too can have an impact on one's life. Poverty taught me life lessons. Such as, going after what you want, working hard, and to never look for a handout. I always tell others I am humble because I know what it feels like to have a little and I know what it feels like to have a lot. God is going to be with me either way because if I did not have a dime to my name, which was not too long ago, I would still thank Him for who He is and what he did for me. Sending His son to die on the cross for my soul while I was still living in sin. That is indeed love, insurmountable.

I am in no way deserving of this type of love, but You have mercy on me. You gave me a second chance, and I will always be grateful for that. How wonderful, caring, and loving You are? With the world being upside down, I still find a way to smile. I know that I must worship You forever, and stay connected to You because, without You, I am nothing but a lost soul. A tree that has no roots. I need You every step of the way. Lord, Like Solomon, help me be wise. Help me speak words of encouragement that will build people up. Help me teach others in a way they would understand. Use me like you used Jeremiah. All in all, I declare healing over my family. I believe that even if I do not see it in my family now, I may see it in the years to come with my children or my children's children, but it will happen.

I love when I start my mornings off with God. It is such a wonderful feeling to talk to God and sit in His presence. After reading the daily devotional for today, I have learned that it is not okay to judge others for being hesitant about doing something that may be easy for me but challenging for them. I am currently sitting at Trish and Jim's house dog sitting for them. I cannot wait to get my house built. Trish has a beautiful home. When you walk through the doors, it screams peace. I love it here, besides the dogs waking me up at 6:11am to go outside. She has a pool and everything, Trish is so sweet. My coworkers got upset because I had to leave work early to let the dogs out and said I should have just told Trish no. I would never do that to her. It is called loyalty and friendship. Trish is my massage therapist, but she was my shoulder to lean on before I had a personal therapist. She helps me out so much and I am thankful for her. I love her and Jim. Today I told Trish my story and she said I could write a book. I was thinking to myself, if only she knew what I had planned.

3AM THINKING ABOUT SUCCESS AND ACTING

ON IT 3:11am Trish House

It is literally 3am in the morning, and I am awake. It is crazy how I was beyond tired after practice today and still could not fall asleep. I felt like I was waking up every hour tossing and turning. For some reason, I always dream a lot, but this morning was different. I woke up at 1:20am and went on my phone but thank God I removed social media last Sunday, so I would not be distracted.

Normally I listen to Joel Osteen, but something said to go to T.D. jakes app. On the app, I went through the sermon notes section and I always try to find something relevant to what I am experiencing now. So, I started from his very first sermon in January of this year and then scrolled until I found one titled, "Coming into Focus." I knew it was for me. You know how you are looking for something and then you find it and your spirit agrees, yep that just happened! It is almost like I woke up hungry or thirsty looking for something to fill me up. Well I did eat two lemons, but seriously this is just what I needed. Sometimes we think we are focused on the right things, but we are really focused on things that do not matter. The sermon talked about trying to receive new blessings with old habits and Lord knows this is something I was struggling with. Everything seems intentional.

In church, the lessons have been about reframing our mind, walking in favor and putting off the old self. I know that I am transitioning, I can feel it. Growth hurts, it is not easy at all and on some days, I do not know how I made it through. Made it through the morning, the workouts, the weights, the meal prepping and just everyday life in general. The other day I was literally praying while running. People assume that this sport is hard, but hard is not even the word I would use to describe it. You must be made for it. I cannot say it any other way. It is hard waking up every day knowing your body is sore, but also knowing that there are thousands of athletes around the world doing the same thing. I want it and I am motivated by the struggle and there is something inside of me that will separate me from the rest. Truth be told, we all want success, right? I am learning something new every single day. I know it is not in my strength, but God is real. I have goals and dreams, but even if God sees fit to use me another way for His glory then I am okay with that as well because the journey is worth it. I am no longer looking back, like Paul, I am moving forward. Who starts their day at 3:27am on a Saturday morning? I did. He woke me up to spend time with Him and it was a moment I longed for. Keep the faith is what I continue to tell myself. Even when God seems far away, He is always there, if that makes sense. He will take the pain away. He literally restored my soul. He always shows me which way I need to go. I love the Lord! Sometimes we can miss our moments with Him by being lazy or not being awake.

My eyes are open now both physically and spiritually.

-

Believe it, Act on it, Live it

The Perfect Race

There is no such thing as the perfect race. It does not exist. In fact, there is only one perfect person who has walked this earth and I am sure you are aware of who I am referring to. Perfect: meaning free from any flaw or defects. While being a professional runner, I can surely claim Team USA, but I am truly running for Team G.O.D. He is my official team sponsor. Now, here is my question to you: who are you doing it for and why do you go so hard? Why do you work long hours at the job you are currently at and what are you looking to get out of it? This can be applied to almost any area in your life. Knowing the who and why are so important to reaching your destination. I had to tell myself that this is not where my race ends. To be quite honest, I was thinking about throwing in the towel. In my mind, I was done. I was looking at everyone else's situation and thinking, when will it be my turn. I asked God, have I not struggled enough? Have I not sacrificed enough? Have I not been strong my entire life? But then I remind myself, who am I to question the one who knows my past, present, and future.

Something amazing happened last night. I received a direct message (DM) from a new friend/sister in Christ, and she asked if she could have fifteen minutes of my time. I was reluctant at first, but then hey why not, I am up late anyways. The phone rings, and I am nervous as all outdoors, not knowing how the conversation was going to go. She begins to speak as if she had known me her whole life. After minutes, which eventually turned into hours, I slowly feel my spirit being uplifted as we laughed and talked about her old college experience. The next part is what caught my attention. She asks me a simple question, and I responded with my normal indecisive, self-blaming thoughts. She goes on to say, "Be still." That was my third-time hearing or seeing that message within one week. So, I thought okay, I am still. I have been waking up every morning, and my phone is set to do not disturb until noon each day, I am still for sure. She says, "No. Alexis, be quiet, listen. Your problem is that you talk too much. You talk your way out of situations and your blessings. You are a control freak, just stop it right now and listen to the small voice." At that moment, I had never felt so convicted in my life. It made perfect sense, I prayed, but I was expecting God to answer me one way without truly acknowledging who He is. He can send confirmation through a stranger, but me being Alexis, I was not quick to trust the words of strangers.

As my new friend went on to explain how one would know if a confirmation or word is coming from the Father, I listened. If the person on the other end is speaking directly on your situation without ever knowing the details, it was coming from God. In the past, I have had some ah-ha moments, but not like this one. This was an eye-opener. It was confirmation in so many ways. The Alexis who thought she knew it all, did not know anything at all and I am not afraid to say that. I need to stop over-thinking, say yes to my Father, and be still. Three simple, yet effective, instructions for living the life I would love. Lesson learned: a fifteen-minute conversation that turned into one hour and thirteen minutes can be a blessing in disguise. I said yes! I will continue to say yes!

All the days of my life, I want God to be in control. Who

said it was my job to figure everything out on my own? No one. God is truly blessing me and opening doors right before my eyes. I have gone to everyone, but Him in the past. I know it is time to take my faith and trust to another level concerning my father. He is so alive and real. He works through people. I am going to fast this week and really sit in His presence so that I will know when to move. Right now, I do not see a way, but I know that God is always making a way. Trusting God when I cannot trust myself is a lesson learned today. I love God very much. I only want to make Him proud and live right. This week's task is simple: Listen. It is already done. So now that I got somewhat of a lecture and lesson. It is time to unwind and relax.

Now I am sitting out by the pool at my favorite table. You know, the one with the small stone pattern that everyone seems to have in their backyard at cookouts. Any who, I am super excited about today! I am not sure if I woke up on the right side of the bed or what, but I feel good! I mean I am up and dressed for practice at 7am, shoot that is one hour early for me. After listening to Joel Osteen's message this morning titled "Drop It," I realized I might be holding on to past offenses and hurt, even a bit of bitterness and I do not want to feel or be that way. God willing, I have too much life to live to not be happy and be everything He wants me to be. I want to be like Paul and forget what is behind me and look forward to what is ahead. I am going back to my hometown this weekend to be with my family. I know I will be at peace and excited when I see everyone's faces. Sometimes I think I focus on what could go wrong instead of focusing on what could possibly go right. I always look forward to watching my nephew's open their Christmas presents and getting some of grandma's good soul food; it does taste like food from the soul. I look forward to hearing my mom walk into the house and filling the room with her Mississippi accent. Originally, I was going to stay in Clermont, where I train so that I can volunteer somewhere locally. However, I can also do that back in my hometown. God has been blessing me, and I want to show the world, but maybe this time I will move in silence. He always has a plan to work everything out for my good. I am just humbled that He chose someone like me out of everyone else in the world. My heart is really at peace. I am forever thankful.

When I have time to sit and think, I realize my problems are not as bad as they seem. I have taken time to evaluate everything that has been said to me up until this point. From now on, I will use it to grow. Grow as a Christian, grow as an athlete, and grow as a person. The hurt is real, but my God is bigger and greater. The enemy will not stop, but I know God has my back. Tough times come to make me stronger. God never leaves my side. I will not quit. Quitting is not an option. It just amazes me how God can turn your entire day around. During my time home, I had the opportunity to sit with and distribute toys to children at the hospital. It was nice to see the smiles on those kids' faces. I met two little girls named Lexie, which was cool because their name was like mine and I felt a connection there. Murielle brought a Ninja Turtle with her and the boy she gave the gift to had not smiled in three weeks. Well, guess what, on this day, that little boy smiled. This is so awesome! I learned a valuable lesson there. It is not about how much you have, it is about what you do with what you have. I am grateful. Having a little or having a lot, I still have God, and that is enough It is almost time for Christmas. It feels good to be up and getting in the word. Moments like this make me happy, and I feel at peace. Even the simple joys of sitting outside and listening to nature. It a great feeling to be around family and to stay up late night having talks about any and everything under the sun. These moments are what I have longed for all my life. To be honest, I am just in a good mood overall. No gift or amount of money can take that away. Thank *You, God, thank You for allowing me to have this quiet journal session with You, openly and freely.*

I stop expecting gifts on Christmas but what I want on today, no gift can overshadow. I mean everything. I did not want anything for Christmas but to be with my family and have a nice home-cooked meal. We ate at grandma's house around three in the afternoon, as usual, then I went to do a quick photo-shoot at the Green Bridge and finished the day with my dad. The family even had a few laughs while playing the game Dirty Santa. That is all I ever wanted, was to see my family happy. For years now, I wanted us to feel the love as one big happy family. God is just so amazing! On top of getting to spend time with family, I came home to a bunch of gifts under the Christmas tree. Wow, Trish and Jim strike again! Amazing people who love me so much. I am so thankful to have them in my life. Again, I did not expect a thing from anyone. I realized the significance of just being able to wake up and open my eyes on a day that was not promised. Trish and Jim brought me everything I wanted, literally everything. From fresh homemade pickles to a pickle shirt, and favorite room fragrance plugin. This whole entire time since I have been living with them, which has not even been a year but seems like forever, they have been listening to me. Every little thing I said I wanted, I now have.

Of course, after Christmas comes the closing of a year. The time of the year where everyone writes resolutions that only last for a few months. Hey, to each their own. For some reason, I was lying in bed about to get emotional. Then I jumped up and decided to journal. I guess what triggered that emotion is me looking back at old pictures, realizing that I will not bring some old friends over to the New Year with me. It is all good, but it is sad at the same time. I am not sure if I need new friends or if I just need to focus on the bright side of things. I woke up and typed the full college section of my book. It blows my mind how much I can do when I am alone with no distractions. I am so anxious about going to church on New Years that nothing else matters. I do not care much about going out or drinking. I just want to eat dinner and head to church, start the year off right. I like where I am in life right now, but I know I can always be better. I am thankful.

Taken by Him

So here we are! A new journal, New Year, new me! No, I am joking about the "new me" part, but I do want to share my personal journal entries from this year. I want to share how life has been since I fully surrendered and allowed myself to be taken by Jesus completely. My day usually starts with me reading the word and when I read the word, I feel an extra boost of energy from somewhere. I feel like I am ready to take on whatever the present day should offer. God is so good, and I must stay rooted in Him then everything else will follow. Like the courageous Joshua, in the Bible, it is my secret formula.

As I enter the first week of a new year, I wanted to try something different. The church I attend is having a corporate fast, so I participated. I am on day two of my 40 day fast and miracles are happening right before my eyes! I received a call from the manager at the Chiropractor's office I have been going to for three years. The manager proceeds to say, are you able to start work this Wednesday? Wow! I was blown away. I had started my fast on Saturday, and here it is Monday, and I am already seeing God work. For three months, I have been looking for a part-time job or at least something to cover my expenses outside of funds from track meets. A job that would not be too strenuous and work with my track schedule. It was perfect. Just like that, God provided. I am so grateful. He works so swiftly. While I was recently in my hometown church, Pastor Nic said something would happen this week around 1pm today. Well for me, it happened at exactly 5:08pm, and that is good enough for me. I mean God literally opened that door for me. He says no sometimes to give us better later. *God, You are so good and faithful. I am so sorry for doubting You.* Blessings follow obedience. What I am experiencing now must be faith on another level.

I am learning so much in this season. They are what I would like to call, life lessons. Here are a few, if someone is rude to me, bless them, smile and keep moving forward. It is simply meekness under control. Do not give away my power! Keep my strength under control. Remember the garbage truck rule concerning what we allow others to dump on us. It must stop. I do not have to accept anyone else's garbage. Please know that God gives me the strength to go through challenges with a good attitude. The enemy will use anything against. Nothing is off limits. However, I have a declaration I proclaim on days when the enemy tries to attack. This is the day the Lord has made. I will no longer wait until tomorrow comes to be happy. I will not wait for people to change. I am happy right now, at this moment. I am thankful. I am blessed. I am accepted. I am beautiful. I am capable. I am chosen. I am loved. I am redeemed. I am healed. I am filled with joy. I have peace. I am wonderfully made. I am a child of the God.

After having a good night of cleansing and freeing my mind, I knew the next day was going to be even better. I woke up and tried to eat some wheat cereal. That cereal was not cutting it, so I made scrambled eggs and then for the first time in a long time, sat in the closet. It is so funny because I literally bunched my clothes together on the top row of the closet to make a small space in the bottom, to sit in God's presence. It is amazing what five or ten minutes in His presence will do. It turned my morning around. I read up to chapter fifteen in the book of John. It is crazy how Jesus knew Judas would betray him and that Peter would deny him. I do not know what I would do if I knew one of my friends would betray me, but then again it was for the glory of God. I know this one thing, I love God and will keep His commandments. He will not leave me as an orphan. In John 14:14, Jesus says, "If you ask in my name, this I will do. "Whoever believes in Him will do the work He does. That is why I am on a different mission at this point of my life. My finish line looks different from everyone else's. For years or even my whole life, I have been running a race, tired and weary, not knowing which direction to go. Yes, indeed, life is a marathon and a sprint, but even in a marathon, you must know the direction that you are going in or the race will not serve its purpose. Finally, I have figured out part of my purpose, so this gives me the confidence I need to keep running, boldly. I am glad I chose to start this day off right by getting in the word. I love the Lord. When I get in the word, I can see his beautiful creation. I can look beyond the natural and see the supernatural. I can speak encouraging words to others. I can be more Christ-like. Even looking up and seeing the clear skies assures me that the Lord with me.

I remember when I sat in the closet years ago, but it was for a different reason. I used to sit in a dark closet to weep. It was different from the regular cry, I felt my soul crying out in those times. I was hurt. Now everything is different, I have a new life. I am doing much better with handling my problems. I do not get all worked up like I used to. It is not worth it, especially if I am praying about it then I should not worry about it. My verse for today is John 16:33 "in this world you will have trouble but take heart I have overcome the world."

In this season, my sister in Christ, Kiara and I are starting a women's ministry, Sisters of Royalty. It will be centered on the theme: rejected by them, selected by Him. Though the world may reject you, God still loves you and has selected you to move forward with Him while being predestined for greatness. I am excited! This is huge for us as young Christian females who have struggled in life with depression, guilt, shame, insecurities, and other issues. I sometimes struggle with staying on top of my father's work, but I know it must be done. Little things like having time to journal, having my work clothes out and ready, having my snacks packed, and going over a verse or two helps me to do better. All in all, I am thankful no matter what. No one can take my joy away. God reveals everything to me at the right time. Isces, my lash extension expert, did my lashes last night at her new place and of course, we had church, as always. She said her mother-in-law said that we must be careful about whose voice we are hearing because the enemy will speak to us too. That caught my attention because I have never thought of it in that way. You really must be on guard always. I realized the enemy does not want me to be great. Just the other night, two Angels entered my room and told me that I will accomplish everything I want to accomplish with God's grace. His grace is what I need to move forward. I needed to hear that. I was afraid at first when they entered my room, but I thank God for that confirmation. I am really in tune with my spiritual side. My soul is at peace; His grace is what I need to move forward. I needed to hear that now, it is time for me to head to track practice!

Speaking of practice, practice has been going well. I am learning how to open my stride, I am running hills the right way and making all the times I need to work out. All glory to God for giving me the strength and ability to be victorious. He has placed some amazing people in my life to help me on this journey. I really need guidance on everything, but from Him. I have more stuff to work on, and I am going to get it done. I want my will to be lined up with God's will. His will be done. I want His ways, His love, and His everything. He is so good to me even when I am not good to Him. Silly me for thinking I knew what was best for me. Everything that looks good is not good for you. Temptation is always knocking at the door wanting me to mess up, but I will not do it, and I will not get discouraged.

Being discouraged will only keep you down. So, what I do now is reverse psychology. If fear, doubt or anything that is not of God tries to come my way, I fight it with the word. When I do this, I can see how things are working in my favor. Trust me, I have been in a place where I thought everything was going wrong as if I was a magnet for bad things waiting to happen. Looking forward, I am so excited about what God is doing in my life! I have never felt better about my future. He is a promise keeper, and I know I can always count on Him. Yesterday morning, Dr. Rhode sent me a word from the Lord, she says that He says He has not forgotten about me and He has something in store for me. I could hardly keep my composure. Let me remind you, this happened shortly after I sat beside a couple I met in this new church, and boy were they happy to see me. I am now attending Hope International Church, and everything is perfect here. You can feel the love in that place. Something special happened after church service, a lady by the name of Whitney from the praise and worship team prayed for me after church. I just love how she thanked God for my feet, and she prayed that this year will be my year. As I sit back and read the book of Romans and think about Abraham and his strong faith, I know I must believe the same way and know God has the power to do what He says He will do. My track practices are going great. I am getting better at the longer workouts and I am no longer panicking when coach tells us our times. Everything is well. Kiara and I are really pushing the Sisters of Royalty movement for the church, I am so glad God chose us to work together to do work for His kingdom. When I sit down and look at everything, I realize how blessed I am. I was speaking to a close friend earlier who recently lost his mom, and I can only imagine the pain that he feels inside. I just want to be there for him. Often, people will say they feel what you are going through or can sympathize, but I believe no one truly knows or feels your pain unless they are experiencing what happened first-hand. Losing someone is one of the hardest things to cope thing.

All I should say is, God is real! He is faithful, and He hears all prayers, even the short, quick ones. I love Him so much. He can turn things around fast, I mean in a matter of seconds, minutes, and in my case today, hours. I had my mind made up, I was done with a certain situation and person, but God sent them right back to me. That just goes to show, when we do things in our own power or without God, He will make a way even when we say we are done. I am full of joy and feel complete again. For some reason, it is hard for me to accept when people come in and out of my life. Especially if it is tied to something in my childhood, and I do not like that feeling of abandonment. I love my Father in heaven and I know He loves me. I know that even when others walk out on me, He will never leave me nor forsake me

It all makes sense, how we must learn to love and more importantly, learn to love the way Christ loves. I wonder why it works like that. We naturally sin and lie at a young age and those things were never taught to us. Are we natural born sinners? That is so deep. The other night, a Wednesday night bible study, the topic was on loving people but not loving what they did or what they have done in the past. Love is hard work. Since Valentine's Day, I have been in a bit of a mood about being single, but I realize I was focusing on my circumstances or current situation and not focusing on my God. He gives me the best love, Agape love. This past week has shown me some things. Love never ends. My faith is measured by how far I am willing to go for that person or thing I truly want. Real love stays through adversity. Real love looks beyond your own feelings and emotions. Real love builds. It is scary to choose the wrong person or things and operate outside of God's will. The funny thing about that statement is that the right thing was always present. I know I must love God more than anything else.

Life really is a journey. I love it so far. I remember when things used to stress me out. The old Alexis used to panic about everything, but the difference is that now I truly believe God has my back. Which I am sure this was always the case, but I was too stubborn to see it and believe it. Short praise break, just when I thought I was left behind God sent Ashley Mitchell to help me out. She calls me sis but when she says it, I know it is not coming from a place of being fake. She really does look out for me. To know her story of being born and raised in little Rubonia, FL and has now made a living for herself in Texas is amazing. I am not saying this because she is the person to call on when things get rough, but I am saying this because although she is not my blood sister although she treats me like one. God knows who I need in my life and when I need them. It is like God already knows the outcome. I should trust Him always. The best is yet to come. I cannot complain. As a matter of fact, I will not complain this time around.

In the past, I remember when I wished things were different and complained about everything. Now, instead of doing that, I journal about it and talk to the Lord. I told myself if I do not do anything else, I must journal. It is where I find peace. One thing I have stopped doing is rushing my time with the Lord. It is crazy how at one point this journal was the only thing that kept me alive and now, since I have found joy, I am fighting to keep this journal alive. I have so many good things going for me that I can hardly keep up. God is good. I look back over my life and see how far He brought me, and I am thankful for the good and the bad. Dr. Paul said he had a prophecy for me, but he does not want to be the one to say it because I may doubt it coming from him, and he is not qualified in that area. Nonetheless, I believe in God to do amazing things in my life this season. I was having a conversation with Jim and he said it is all about having the right attitude in life. He also told me to do what needs to be done because no one else is going to do it for me or at least I should not expect them to. He said we can accomplish our desired goal because we woke up on another day that was not promised. Yesterday could have been our last day. And of course, I immediately started to think, but God! Nevertheless, I am thankful for it all. My God is awesome. Let's see what the Lord has in store for me before I fly out to Dallas, Texas.

I get so excited about traveling! It is just something about traveling and being able to enjoy a different environment. I woke up early to make sure I was on time for the fight. To be honest, I am ready to get there. Although it is a business trip for track, I know I will have fun. As I sit here on the plane, I go into deep thought about how God strategically placed people in my life throughout different seasons. Literally everywhere I go I make friends and people adopt me as if I was their own family, and everything always works out. As far as relationships goes, I am happy all by myself. I do not have time for that right now. God is working things out for me and I know everything will go per His plan. Sometimes I feel anxious because I want to know what is going to happen before it does, but I guess that would not be trusting God completely. At this point, I cannot afford to let anyone or anything to steal my joy. This is something I must keep in mind every day. The world certainly did not give it to me and the world cannot take that away. Jim and Trish are really rooting for me. I can tell they love me, and it is pure. Coach Dennis always says, "Do not think about how far away you are, think about how close you are." I mean come on, with God and a new mindset, my whole world changed drastically this year. Regarding track, my personal life, working and just everything in general. The new church I attend is very supportive of my career and I could not have prayed for a better pastor. For a long time, I thought the struggle would be the only thing familiar to me but now I see how God always had a plan. It was necessary. It was necessary for me to go through everything I had gone through, from early childhood until now. But grace, grace is what I had available this whole time.

am still in Texas and having a good time. I figure I would spend time with my sister and niece while I am here on this business trip. We went to the movies and had a girls' night out, which was exactly what I needed. It reminded me of the time I lived with her in Texas before I decided to move to Florida. Though I felt like I was failing there, when I look back, I realize I was making progress. Even this morning's daily devotional opened my eyes to something new. I am reminded that even during the busy times of the day, I need to be aware of God's presence. It is said that we will make better decisions when He is on our minds. The verse that stood out to me was Romans 8:28, "And we know that all things work together for the good of those who love God and are called according to his purpose." The word is powerful. Just reading the word 'beloved' does something to my soul. I feel as though the Lord is speaking directly to you and me. It makes us feel special and set apart.

Another daily devotional also talked about the story of Samson and how he could have saved himself many times. It talked about the importance of avoiding sin and not flirting with it. I can relate to Samson all too well. I am guilty of trying to set boundaries within myself instead of avoiding sin altogether. Like Samson, if I would take heed to all the warnings, then maybe, just maybe, I can save myself some heartache. Like Samson, my passion for certain things was stronger than my will to please God. I cannot lie, the word hurts at times because I feel convicted, but it is much needed for correction. I reminds me that I am not there yet. I am not perfect. This is a scary truth because I have found myself in the same situation time after time, but now I can say I am wiser and stronger. I would love to say I learned my lesson, but temptation is always present. Overall, I feel good, and this Dallas Trip to the Michael Johnson performance center was what I needed. They tested every muscle in my body and gave me insight on things sports related. I had no idea about a lot of things and the people I am with are basically taking care of me. I am blessed! I thank God for bringing me here. A little bit of faith is what I need. I used my work check to get here, and everything worked out just fine. 2017 will be one of the best years of my life. I look forward to it!!

Some laughed. I kept talking. They watched, I kept running. They doubted, I kept preserving. Sometimes you must be your own supporter. Work for it. Certain issues will always be there. It is life, but you should see the good in every situation and keep pressing forward. I knew at some point I would have to do better, and by doing better, I mean make better decisions. One of my biggest fears is not being successful. Now it is time for me to return to Florida and put in serious work.

I usually stay at my brother AJ's place if I have a flight at a crazy time. He lives close to the airport, so it was always convenient. I could not have asked for a better morning. I woke up to my 2-year old niece Aubrie in my face and her pet dog, Duke. I say it is her dog because she thinks it is. Although it was only 7am, I was okay with the fact that Duke stood in my face and did not lick me. I would have had an instant attitude about that. Seeing Aubrie's face gave me the motivation I needed to get up and do a workout. I was feeling sluggish after the workout, so I decided to clean my brother's whole entire apart. Between cleaning and my obsession with pickles, I have found what soothes my soul. It makes me happy. Peace and quiet at the beginning of the day with a bit of worship music always does the trick. God is so good to me. I cannot begin to describe how I feel. He is always one or two steps ahead of me. I am looking forward to the day when I have my own place. I can see it now with my religious wall art, candles burning in my prayer room, clean, cozy and smelling good. I know I will get there if I stay close to God. I am loved. I am a daughter of the King. I know that my father looks at my heart and not the outside appearance. I will continue to guard my heart so positive things can continue to flow and from it. I will spend today exploring nature, sit outside, and enjoying the creation.

I can hardly believe it is already the month of March and so many great things are happening already. Who knew I was going to work at a Chiropractor's office? The same chiropractor that I have seen for three years now. The staff here is amazing, and I am so glad Dr. Paul chose me to work here. I know if I just keep working hard, the world will see God's hard work. I must remember even when things are going in the right direction to thank Him. At first, I was not sure how everything was going to work out, but now I see that God is always on time. Through all the trials, I did not give up and I will never give up. I remember it all. I will never forget. I went from being in Texas and working in the footwear department at Dick's Sporting Goods to working the 4am shift at Old Navy, to being a collection specialist on defaulted payday loans, to working until 10pm at a grocery delivery service, and now having flexible hours. I can leave work in time to make Bible Study and that is a major blessing to me. It is not about the work itself, it is about having the flexibility I did not have until this job. Again, God knew I needed Dr. Paul in my life for more than being a chiropractor, but a brother in Christ as well. I could not think of another doctor that has laid hands on me in prayer while I sat in their office. Dr. Paul is open with it, he has no shame about caring for his brothers and sisters in Christ, and I need to be around people like him. Very successful businessman, but a man of God first is how I would describe Dr. Paul. He is one to really give you the shirt off his back if you need it and then will turn around to say, "It is my pleasure to serve." I am so grateful to have met Dr. Paul.

After a long day of work at the office, I came home to a bag of sweet potatoes in the freezer. Of course, Trish tells me I can have them, so I can save the ones I recently bought. Gosh, both she and Jim make my life so much easier. I do not know where I would be this year if they did not open their home to me. It a coincidence how everything starts to work out when you focus on the right things and by focus, I mean total focus. It has been a long time coming. Staying focused and taking time out for myself was the key. Even when I have days where I feel off and distant from God, I have a friend like Jessica to remind me to pray and talk to God. It is funny because she sent that reminder to me at 2am when she was in the club. I am saying that to say this, you can be a blessing to someone wherever you are if you consider the big picture. Although I knew Jessica through sports at Murray State and we are college buddies, she is now a sister to me. I am gaining more sisters than anything. Though I am the baby on both sides of my family, I am gaining new family members from all over. No, I am not confusing this with being gullible and friendly, but I feel that God is creating a shift in my life. God shows me how he can give me more than what I asked. Yes, my family is loving, and I will continue to thank God for them. Family is family. God chose mine, and I will continue to do my part in mine.

Until I see a change, I will be obedient to my calling. Whether it is serving in my family, church or community, I am up for the task. Now I am ready to see what this new day has to offer. It seems like a normal day. Practice then work. I met a lady named Christie today through Dr. Paul. He asked me to meet her downstairs, and said she had a word for me. I had no idea what this concerned but figured she had kids and she wanted me to speak to them. Sure, why not? I walked into the room, and she asked if she could pray for me, and of course, I said yes! I began to cry halfway through the prayer. It was not until the end when I realized she had prophesied to me and it came directly from above. God really does love me. She talked about things I knew no one else knew except God because these were the things I prayed about in my quiet time. I was reminded to go back to why I started running in the first place. It was fun for me and relaxing at the same time. She told me not to settle and that God says that I am His princess and I should have the best. I am paraphrasing, but it all made sense. I am so glad God did not forget about me. He sends confirmation when feel I like He is not listening, or I am alone. I had never met this lady a day in my life, and she sent a word directly from the Father. I feel so relieved now. For weeks, I have been restless and unsettled. I felt like something was off. Through it all, as imperfect as I am, He still loves me. There have been many times when I was humbled and brought to my knees, but I know it was all out of love. We all need that at times. He has made my failures work out for me in the past. So, to think of it, failures are not really failures, it is a step towards pursuing my goals. I see everything as a potential gain. I have worked on myself, I have kept the faith, and I have preserved. To me, that is what success is all about. I am one step closer to my goals.

I recently found an editor to help with my book but let me not take all the credit. My mentor, Pat Williams, co-founder of the Orlando Magic has helped me tremendously. He has written over 100 books and is currently working on another book. I never thought, in a million years, I would be connected to such influential people who pour into my life in such a loving way. From the dreams to the visions that come to me in the middle of the night when I cannot sleep, it is all unbelievable. Little Alexis has grown up to become an encourager, a speaker, and professional athlete. If I had never fully believed in God growing up, I sure as heck believe Him now. I cannot make these miracles happen on my own, are you kidding me? Just the other night, I had a dream I laid hands on a little girl in the hospital who had a brain disease and she was immediately healed. Then I met a lady in my dream shortly after who was selling shirts with the same quotes I had written in my journal. There are just certain things I am passionate about, like helping single moms. Maybe it relates somewhat to my strong sisters in my immediate family who are caring for my nephews and nieces or something God put in my heart, but either way, the passion is there. I always notice how the single moms in my hometown commend me for being great on the track, but I look to them as if they are the true soldiers. I know when the time comes, I will have so much to learn about being a mother and after seeing some of the struggles in a family when one parent is absent, I know I need a husband. I need a helper. Call it a fairytale life if you want, but I want to do this the right way, marriage then kids. No, I am not saying it will all be easy with a husband, but from what I have heard it will be a little easier when you are not the only one waking up in the middle of the night to quiet the baby. My heart longs to have a little girl, but I know it is all in God's timing. I will continue to focus on this season of life.

I have a little more time before I can think about having a little one of my own. For now, I am going to focus on my first love, my baby, track and field. The first meet of the season is next week!! Jacksonville here I come! I ran in Jacksonville, Florida years ago. So, I texted Coach K, my college coach to see if he remembered. He responded back quickly and said, of course, he remembers because on that same track is where things started to turn around for me. This gave me all the confidence in the world going into next week. I was thinking to myself, I know the track, I found a hotel at the last minute, and the weather is great. I got this! The feeling of excitement that day caused me to have dreams about the old college days on the track at Murray State. When things started off rough but ended up working in my favor.

Now from all the dreaming and reminiscing, it is here, the first track meet of this season. I am excited!! God knew what He was doing by sending me here. He sure did. I had so many dreams last night that I cannot remember them all. I am sitting in the hotel room, in Jacksonville and thought about what changed when I was performing at my best. Two things, I believed in God without a doubt, and I believed in myself. God gave me the strength and power every time. God can bless me right where I am. I find myself guilty of trying to find a special place to speak to God or feel His presence. I know that even if I am not praying on my knees, He still hears my heart. Today, I am not thinking about how I feel, but I am keeping my eyes focused on the Lord and who He is. I remember a dream I had recently about Dwyane Wade, a professional basketball player. He was sitting in the TV room at my grandma's house. He called an Uber then we walked outside together. He stopped me in mid-sentence when I told him I was twelve-years-old when I started running track and I would have never thought I was going to be a professional runner. He looked at me and said, "decide what you want and do not get so easily distracted with what is going on around me." He said he wanted to make a certain salary and that was his number one goal, and he did that. He told me to make up my mind about what I want. No more indecisiveness. Let me say this, I do not know D. Wade personally and I have never met him, but I do know of his accomplishments in the sports world, and he seems like the type of guy that would give good advice from one athlete to another. Dream or not, I took it to heart. I made up my mind. No more second-guessing, the time is now. Some dream huh? Maybe it was the fact that I fell asleep thinking about success but whatever the case may be, I hear you loud and clear D. Wade.

From one night of vivid dreams, I woke up feeling focused, relaxed, and rejuvenated. Aside from the fact that I won one race and placed second in the other, I am still making progress. It is still early in the season and I must learn to leave the misfortunes on the track and grow from them. It is a new day, I am sitting out by the pool with Trish and Jim watching a show, "This is us" and enjoying life. Sundays for me are always filled with the word, cooking, cleaning, and rest. One thing I did differently on this Sunday was leave my phone inside during family time. I felt free and could get a lot done on my iPad even while watching the show. I must be consistent with doing these things on a regular. Most people seem to think I have things all figured out, but, truth be told, I still struggle with things daily.

It is not by mistake that I named this section, Taken by Him. I need to be taken by the Lord, in an intimate relationship with Him and connected to Him. As I sit out by the pool this morning and watch the guys cut down the tree in the neighbor's backyard, I am reminded of something. The enemy tries to cut off all ties with the Lord, but he can never get to the actual root. The God who gives can also take away. But I know this one thing, I am grounded in the Lord, He is my root, my rock, my everything. At times, I do believe God allows me to go without things, like men, friends, family, and money until I am left with Him. You know, the things I have allowed to become distractions in my life. I guess we can call those things dead leaves. I have learned something new here. At times, certain people in our life will not serve us any good purpose and it is our responsibility to either water those things or simply cut them off. The question I ask myself: what branches are on your tree and are they throwing shade or helping you elevate and grow closer to achieving your goals? No more second guessing, just cutting. This is just what I needed to hear before my next track meet

The next track meet is at the University of Florida. So here I am, in Gainesville, sitting in an apartment that is somewhat like the one I had at Murray State. As soon as I walked in, I had flashbacks of when I was in college. The track meets, the parties, the late studying, everything. I am thankful that the Pastor's son, TJ McCoy was kind enough to let me stay there so I did not have to book a hotel. As I sit in the guest room listening to TJ laugh at funny videos on his iPad, I was reminded to relax, breathe, and have fun. God has a sense of humor for sending me daily reminders. All I need to do is execute and run my race. To pass the time later, I am thinking of writing a list of things that I am thankful for. For my daily devotional, I read a passage on David. To be honest, I think David is one of my favorite characters in the Bible. He was obedient and did everything to obtain God's glory. He pressed forward when he did not fully understand the outcome. He trusted God would be with him every step of the way. Even for myself, I did away with things that were spoken over my life in my early childhood. Although I was hurt in the past, that does not mean I should live hurt forever. Lord, thank You for showing me that You are top priority in my life. Everything I do, I do it for You. I run to the finish line for You. You never let me down, and now it is time for me to do my part and finish well. Lord, with Your strength, I can do anything, I believe the promise You gave me, and I can feel that You are doing a new thing in my life. Lord be with me and help me remain calm on the track. I want to run in such a way to obtain the prize. Amen. This is my prayer the night before race day.

I am awake at a decent time after a full nights' rest and I am ready to run. It is race day! I am running the 100meter, 200meter, 4by1 and 4by2 relay race all in one weekend over the next two days. I am ready, this is what I trained for! As I sit in the warm-up area listening to music, I can feel my soul being calmed to the words of Kevin Levar's song, "Your Destiny" and "Don't Give Up" by Yolanda Adams. It is amazing what one or two songs can do. Today I am running the 200meter which is my favorite race. If I attack the curve just right, it gives me the momentum I need to finish the last 100 meters strong. As I walk over to the starting line, I am calm and ready. After fighting to get in the race because I was told I entered the wrong section online, I found favor with the meet officials. I am running in lane 2, but hey that does not matter. I am ready. The guns go off! POW! I can feel every one of my steps, I am swinging my arms back and forth as if they were my weapons, and I come off the curve and notice I am not in first place. What did I do, I changed my form, I got tense? I approach the finish line, and I am 5th place. I cross the line with utter disappointment. What just happened? Was I overly confident? Was I too relaxed? Did I do something wrong or is this where I am supposed to be my second meet of the season. So many thoughts running through my head. Well, there is nothing to do now but take a cool down lap and go back to TJ's apartment to get ready for the relays tomorrow. I cannot understand why I am so hard on myself. Maybe this track thing is not for me if the season is already off to a bad start, I do not know. I mean I know I said I want to be like David and finish the race, but how? How in the heck do you remain positive when things do not turn out the way you want them to? I need God to teach me how to be kind to myself and have confidence in Him.

Thank goodness, I have a chance to redeem myself. I woke up with a different mindset. Though I did not do as good as I had expected yesterday, I know I must stay focused. Today I have the 100 meter first, then the 4by1 and 4by2 relay. Yesterday was humbling, so I decided to keep to myself and stay in my own little corner before the race with my headphones on. I have the same routine every meet. Find a corner, listen to music, journal a bit, and relax until it is time to warm up. After the warm-up, I find myself back at the starting line. The starter calls the race, "Runners on your mark, set, go." POW! The guns go off, my angles are good, I drive out, stand tall and run through the finish line. In a matter of seconds, the race is over. Much better than yesterday! The time was not blazing fast, but I did improve on something, and that was running through the finish line no matter what. My coach always stresses the importance of running through the finish line. Now I have my confidence back and I am ready for the relays. I ran better than I did in Jacksonville, so I was happy about that. Closer and closer to my goals, I am ready to get the baton in the relay and execute. I am not shocked that I am the anchor leg, I ran the last leg at this same track meet last year. I am not saying that to be arrogant, but I am saying that because I am familiar with it. We are back on the track after practicing handoffs, and I am ready. Adrenaline is going but not so much nervousness, at least I do not think I am. The gun goes off, the crowd is cheering, Veronica takes off like a canon, she passes the baton to Kaylin, Kaylin does her thing and passes it off to Murielle and hear comes Murielle full speed. I am replaying what coach said this past in practice, take off and do not look back because she is going to come at you and not back off the gas. This is all track talk. I see her coming, I am turned to my left looking at her and looking at the mark, she hits the mark, and I turn around to take off, I am stuck, I move forward, and you will not believe what happened next! I find myself on the ground, looking up to watch the other runners finish the race. I tried to get back up as quickly as possible, but I could not. All I could think about was I let three people down who trusted me to finish the job strong. I did the one thing every runner on a relay dreads will never happen. I dropped the stick. My life is over; the world is ending. Okay, I am sure it is not that serious, but at that moment it was. I cannot believe I fell on the track. I was hurt and scrapped up badly, but really, I was more embarrassed than anything. If there was ever a moment I could be invisible, now would be a perfect time to escape. The girls were very supportive. They made sure I was okay and reassured me that they were not upset and things like this happen. Of course, I would expect this from two veterans in the sport, but man I felt bad. I fell off a bike when I was younger, but these scratches hurt worse than that. I will live. I walked over to the medical tent and got everything disinfected and returned to the team tent. Talk about the walk of shame. I went to see Dr. Rhode who made sure my back was okay after I fell and made sure nothing major was injured. She looked at me and said, "Hey, not right now Lex, you have another race to run. A chance to redeem yourself. Get back out there and finish. You got this!" That was everything I needed and more. A friend to say do not beat yourself up about the fall, everything will be okay. Put your big girl panties on right now. I love Dr. Rhode for that. She is also a believer, so she knew exactly what I needed to hear at that time.

I warm up again for the third time today. The 4x2 relay is up next, and again I am the last leg of the relay, bringing it home. I feel confident about everything. I tend to do well when I am upset anyways so let's head over to the track. I am ready for real this time. I walk over to the track, the gun goes off, and I am waiting patiently to get the baton. I know that I have one job and that is the one thing I am focused on. I receive the stick in my right hand, and I take off. Running for my life, not looking to the left or right. The race is over, and I have reached the finish line. Not a first-place finish but I did finish well. I cannot complain about that. Even with the great fall in the 4x1 relay earlier, I can go home with some sort of confidence that the meet was not a total disaster. I cannot understand why I am so hard on myself. Just when I thought I was over what others think of me, I still beat myself up about it. There is nothing left to do now but pack my bags and head home to Palmetto, my hometown, so I can visit with family. As much chaos as I have with my family at times, they love on me like no one else. C'mon, who does not have chaos in their family? The one thing that will make me feel better is riding in the passenger seat of my dad's truck just like the old days when I fell asleep, hoping he would say I could spend the evening with him.

The other thing that brings me peace is attending church. This weekend, I went to my home church, Shining Light Church of God and Christ located in Rubonia, Florida. The pastor blessed me tremendously. His prophecy was to allow God to take me higher and do not resist Him in doing so. Stay in my lane. Extra weight is not good for me whether it is good or bad. This is my personal race of life. God knows my heart and desires. God says, I know what it means to run a race. The same way I train my body physically, I should use that same energy to train my spiritual side. He told me to let it go. Do not look back. It is over. I cannot move forward while looking back. The accident did not cause me any harm. Do not lose heart. God can make it happen. God understands.

Verse mentioned in prophecy: "lay aside every weight that so easily entangles us" -Hebrews 12:1

When I heard this prophecy, I knew it was about the fall this past weekend on the track. The accident or fall was supposed to hurt me, but God will use that very thing and turn it around for my good. I do not see how, but I know He will.

This week in practice will be challenging. I know jokes will be made and everyone will want to know what happened on the track when I fell, and I am not ready for it. Why can't people just let it go? It is like they never remember the good things about you, but they remember all the bad. So here it goes. I knew there was going to be a weird silence, but that is only because I already decided to turn my music on and stay to myself. I have been so worried about how others perceive me that I can barely sleep. Thinking if I am making amateur mistakes like this, then maybe I should give it up.

Maybe this is not the right sport for me. So, we get to the middle of the week, and I can feel something being off on the inside of my heart. I felt as though something was about to happen, but I was not too sure about what was it was. I knew it! Coach pulled me aside for one of those conversations all athletes dread having. Not because he was this big mean guy but if my coach says stay after practice and we need to talk, you immediately start thinking about everything that could possibly go wrong. I was nervous but said a quick prayer and met with coach. To my surprise, it went better than I thought. I felt better after that conversation. It was innocent, peaceful and we ended with a hug. Okay, I did cry an ugly cry, but it was different than the other times I have cried. I felt this sense of peace that I could not put into words. I was afraid more than anything.

At this point, I no longer had a coach. I thought I could coach myself because I have the solid foundation from training during the fall season, but then reality set in. I sent out a mass text message letting my training partners know that I appreciate them, and they were great to work with, and of course a tear fell. It was weird because I could not make sense of why I was crying. My friend, Jeff, called to make sure everything was okay, and he thought it was some big prank. After hearing my ugly cry over the phone, he knew I was serious. I told him I would be okay and hung up the phone. I did not have else anything to say. I knew this was something I only needed to speak to the Lord about. Nothing against Jeff or anyone else but I knew I must say little and do more. I walked into the gym to shower before clocking in at the Chiropractor's office and once again I had a breakdown in the shower. I prayed, *Lord, I know You are behind this some way, somehow. I trust You like I never have before. Please help me. I cannot do this alone. Please help me.* After saying that simple prayer, I walked downstairs to clock in. Trying to fight the tears, while telling everyone I was okay, was one of the hardest things I had to do but it was good for me to go to work because I would have been home with my slow jams on, crying for hours. I made it through the workday. It is time to head home, and I still have a lot on my mind.

The second week of April was one of the hardest times thus far. If you had told me I would part ways with a coach I have been working with for three years, I would have not believed you. There was no argument, no big fight or anything, just a change needed. I knew it was God. When things do not make sense to me, I know God is behind it most times. Talk about walking by faith and not by sight. During this time my close friend Murielle was checking on me periodically. She knows how to check in but not be overbearing, so I love her for that, and most times she knew exactly what to say because she is more experienced in the sport. Again, I kept all comments to myself because I knew I needed to talk to God and God only. Not that she was asking for anything more. God showed me that things may happen in life that I do not understand and often I turn to people before I turn to him. Yea that was enough to make me feel even more down. So, I decided to try something different. I told myself I was not going to worry, and that God would give me exactly what I need. I was playing the waiting game. Hours went by that eventually turned into days, and now it has been exactly one week since I have touched a track or had a coach. I am remaining calm and trusting in the Lord. I am having those thoughts that if I do not get a coach by Sunday then maybe I will start looking into the Criminal Justice field and utilize my degree, but something on the inside is telling me to hold on a little longer.

Sunday comes around and not to sound too depressed but the only thing I look forward to these days is going to church to hear a word. I thought to myself, there must be a word from the Lord today. I attended church, came home, and did the usual Sunday Fun day. I meal prepped for the week, cleaned my room and sat out by the pool with Trish and Jim while working on some things. While watching our favorite television show, HGTV, I received a call. A coach!! Finally, after praying, hoping and wishing, I got the call. That is all I needed to hear. At this point, I did not care if I had ten training partners or one, I was just ready to get back out there. After speaking with the new coach, he explained how my body probably needed that week of rest and relaxation, so I was right on track. I was not out of shape from taking one week off. God is amazing!! I proclaimed I needed a coach and received that call on a Sunday before going into another week. Get this, that was not the only good news I received this week. In the middle of the week, I received a voicemail from a former training partner in Texas. She said USA Track and Field was trying to reach me. I was being smart and said to myself, I do not think I am hard to find, but really my first initial thought was that it was too late. I checked my voicemail at 10pm, and the call was placed early that morning. I returned the call and what do you know, the spot to run on the relay was still open!! I cannot begin to explain the joy I feel inside! I can barely keep my composure throughout the day. I do not think I can even sleep tonight, like how. How did this happen? God is real! My God is real! He did it for me! Alexis Love!! I am famous in my father's eyes. I love God. I have never been this happy before. I am so excited. He makes all things new. I learned after everything I have experienced in the past two weeks, this is a journey with the one who created me. I do not need to worry about tomorrow. When I put my energy towards growing my relationship with Him, everything becomes easier and clearer. I have learned to enjoy His presence in the present. Now here I am, writing my own life story. The little girl who was once in intensive reading classes is now going to be an author. The same person who had trouble comprehending words and phrases in grade school is now publishing a book. I do not know what else to say. My glory outweighs my story for sure. I took a couple of weeks to myself and soaked it all in. The phone call, the joy I have inside, and the thought of representing Team USA on national television is mind blowing.

As I sit on the edge of my bed at the Marriott Hotel located in Downtown Philadelphia, I cannot help but to think about my future. I look at my BIB number for this weekend that reads, "Love USA" and it looks so right. It was somewhat hurtful being overlooked for all these years, but I know in God's timing it is never too late. I also know that at times I was not focused, so it was nobody's fault but my own. I had to put in the work. I cannot expect to be on a relay team if I am not running the times to get there. It takes a deeper level of focus to perform at this level. It takes a certain level of professionalism, but it is not impossible. The experience was overwhelming at first because I had not been on a stage like this in a long time and let alone, gotten television time since college, really. Team USA Blue Team placed third in the 4x1 relay at the 2017 Penn Relays, the largest event in the U.S. and it was unreal. The days leading up to the race were not stressful at all. I was relaxed and went sight-seeing and shopping to pass the time. We had relay practice every morning but had the remainder of the day to ourselves. When it was time to compete, I made sure my heart was in the right place. In the past, I let the lights, noise and everything else consume me but the race. This time, I had total focus. Competing at the Penn Relays was a huge deal because it is the oldest and largest track and field competition in the United States. I did my normal warm-up routine and proceeded to the track. In the big races, you are called on the track early for television purposes but may not run for another fifteen to thirty minutes. My heart was racing all of five minutes, but I quickly reminded myself that I have been here before. As my competitors and I watch the clock for the official start time, the crowd yells "Go Love, USA." What I felt at that moment, words cannot express. The track official came around one last time to make sure we are ready to go. Next thing we hear is the gun, POW! The race is underway. 1st leg, 2nd, 3rd and now the baton is coming towards me full speed. I get ready, foot on the mark and looks for Miki Barber to pass the baton. She passes the baton, smooth handoff, now I am running down the track as if my life depended on it. It took a minute to get my wheels spinning but I finished strong. Considering the fact of not having done much speed work, I ran well. The race was over and immediately after running, my appetite was back. I am certain about being the fastest woman in the world. I will study my opponents, I will put in the work and do whatever it takes. I will not complain. I will be consistent. I will stay humble and continue to work, so when that time comes, I will be ready. The night before my departure flight to Florida, I made a YouTube video. I wanted to share my experience and could not hold it in any longer. Everything was perfect. Nothing is perfect but running at the Penn Relays was nothing short of it. It is what I needed. A little taste of what it was like to put on a Team USA uniform. It was the preview for what is to come. It was everything I once dreamt of. My time in Philadelphia was amazing!

I returned home with overwhelming love and support from my family and fans. Of course, I could not take credit for what just happened. They congratulated me in public, but in private, I gave it back to the Lord. I have so much to talk about in my journal session today. The daily devotion I am currently reading is about speaking the truth in love. I remember having a conversation with my dad about this subject. I asked him if I was doing the right thing about telling the truth about how I started running track. I have questioned myself many times about going against the grain and sharing my secret I kept inside for so long that causes me so much heartache over the years. My dad said these words, "People do not like the truth nor do they like to be judged or make righteous assessments." My dad was right. It was not me; it was the person who has not dealt with their own issues. I am only here to speak about what is right and wrong. On the other hand, I was not going to let it worry me. I was still trying to adjust to everything the Penn Relays brought me. New followers, new opportunities, and new everything. After four years of graduating from Murray state, the head track Coach, Jenny Severns reached out and could get media team to write an article on me. That was another unexpected blessing. The Fellowship of Christian Athletes, an organization I was a part of since high school agreed to do a magazine feature. This was perfect! Blessings on top of blessings. Just when I thought things were getting difficult in my life. I knew I would not get a paper check from running in the relay for a while, so that set me back a bit in bills. Everyone knows that you must run track because you have a passion for it. Most times the checks are delayed, and in this case, I was prepared. Although it set me back, I always have a regular job to fall back on.

On my lunch break, I found two dollars in my car to buy a granola bar from the smoothie shop next door. I walked in with a hand full of coins, trying to hide the feeling of embarrassment. I told the cashier I was getting rid of loose change in my car. She looked at me and said," Alexis, sweetie, do you need food for the week." I looked down and tried to hold back the tears as I walked back to work with my head down. How do I tell her I did not have food after representing Team USA on national television last week? How can I mention this to Trish, Jim, my dad, brother and sister who now lives twenty minutes away from me? No, this is one I must keep to myself. I feel bad knowing everyone has their own life problems and I need help. Honestly, I did not know what I was going to do. I am hanging on by peanut butter, boiled eggs and a prayer. The next day, I walked into work and in the fridge, there was a note inside a bag that read, "for Alexis." Indeed, the lady at the smoothie bar cooked dinner for me. Thank God! Then it just so happened

Megan, my massage therapist went grocery shopping that same week and cleaned out her fridge and cabinets. She asked me to come over for a massage and what do you know, she blessed me with a bag full of grocery. Usually, it is a venting session for me because, like Trish, Megan allows me to be myself and cry on her shoulder. I could not stop crying. Such a humbling experience. Like, who would have ever thought I would be in this situation. Most people will not tell this part of their story, but this is what everyone needs to know. It is not always what it looks like and being a professional athlete is not as easy as it seems. It takes a lot of sacrifice.

I am thankful for the people that are in my life currently. I can see how my future has always been bright. I can hear it in my mentor's voice. Pat Williams is good for putting things into perspective for me. The story goes like this. Alexis Love woke up on competition day. It was somewhat muggy outside, but she did not let that change her level of excitement nor the energy for the day. She put her uniform on the bed, had her famous cup of tea mixed with apple cider vinegar, then proceeded to the corner space to read the daily devotional, *Jesus Always*. After journaling for what seemed like an hour, she was ready to go. Her mind was clear. Ironically, the weather was much better, skies are now clear and were indeed prepared. With her family cheering her on from the sidelines she ran through the finish line, first place. Alexis Love, with a personal best and new world record! She is having the race of her life. Comes home with two first place finishes and a house full of love. Once again, God has her back. Full of surprises and blessings. Hey, a girl can dream, right?

If I could give one piece of advice to a younger individual it would be this, never stop dreaming. I believe in every single one of my dreams. There must be a reason for them. My family, especially my big brothers made sure I stuck with my dreams. Today, I made it my business to call one of them. My brother Courtney made valid points during our conversation. He commended me for staying focused, not having children yet, and not having a man distract me this time around. We talked about religion and how everyone may not be worshipping the same God or believing in the same thing, but we all have the same end goal; success. He reminded me how God showed me what could have happened if I made the wrong turn. I guess the point he was trying to make is that it is okay to be lonely and feel lonely right now in pursuit of my dreams and goals. It is a beautiful thing! We talked about potentially working together to do events and appearances with our products during the busiest times of the year. So, all in all, I had a good day and a great conversation with my big brother whom I have always been fond of. It is amazing to see how God worked everything out for my good. It reminded me to give thanks even when I cannot see the big picture. At first, I was pooped about the delay, but it was for my good. He turned my trials into triumphs. Like my brother said earlier, I know what to do because I came from nothing, we came from nothing, so I know the hard work it takes to get there. I was made for this; I can stand in the sun. God used my hard times to ignite the fire inside of me. Everything that was supposed to harm me gave me the strength to do the impossible.

I think it is funny how I pray for things and ask God to bless me but then when He does, I question it. Like, oh Lord, no this cannot be from You. This situation is too perfect. I did not do anything to deserve this. God has given me the strength to remain focused and keep my eye on the prize throughout all these years. The past couple of months has taught me lessons about family, finances, relationships, jobs, networking and pretty much everything. I have learned that you can never stop growing or working on yourself. Every failure is an opportunity for growth and stability in that area. I have learned that there are times when you will encounter the same situation twice to make sure you have matured in that thing. I have accepted that I can be stubborn, I am a control freak at times, and I used to have a problem with letting things go but I am under construction. I can only continue to evolve from here, right? I am going to continue to grow and live a happy life.

If you would have told me months ago that everything will be alright, I would have laughed. You know it is funny how life turns out. Life is funny. I cannot believe I am going to Ireland!!! Little ol' Alexis!! So many blessings this time around. Everything feels so right. New coach, new training program, new workout regime. Sometimes a change of environment is needed to get you to where you need to be. I believe I needed to be forced out of one situation to get to the next. I stayed in a place too long when God was telling me to leave. But I guess on His own time He removed me when I least expected it. Back to Ireland, wow, who knew? This reminds of a story about Esther in the bible. How God caused the impossible in her life to become possible. He caused miracles to happen, but for me to receive those blessings and miracles, I know I must remove all doubt. Extend my faith, take the limits off and be in position both mentally, physically and spiritually. It has been a tough road, but I know this is my destiny. God put me here. I am not afraid because I have found favor with God. He is amazing for what He does. It is incredible how He works everything out for our good, Romans 8:28. I am sure this is one of my favorite verses because I have mentioned it twice already. My faith is stronger than ever. I am confident, fearless, focused, and most importantly, I am loved by God. When I look back and see how God had His hand on my life, I cannot do anything but smile. I remember when I used to sit in the dark and cry until I could not cry anymore. I know that growing spiritually has helped me all around. The truth used to hurt me, but now the truth has set me free. Even in the home I live in now, I know Trish and Jim love me from the way they look at me when I share good news with them. It feels good to know that I have people who love and support me on this journey we call life. It almost feels like God has given me a fresh start, a new life. Even at the age of twenty-six, I have a new childhood, newfound love and respect for my sport, and I continued writing in my journal but in a different way. I am a motivational speaker with a voice that is no longer quiet, shy or timid.

Yes, I motivate others, but I do have moments where I need to encourage myself. For example, I will be in Canada tomorrow for another meet, and I have this weird feeling inside as if something is not right. This place is familiar. When I feel off, I find myself back in this space. I know what it is. I can put my finger on it. Since I have landed in Guelph, Canada, I have not been in tune with my spiritual side. I am sure you can tell because I did not do my normal routine of journaling on the plane. Do you see how my thoughts just jumped from one thought to the next? Sometimes life is moving at such a fast pace that I forget to journal. Not that Canada was not exciting to travel to, I was not in the mood for it. During competition time, I am so consumed with the race that I forgot to spend time with the Lord. I did not completely forget to meditate but I was not sitting still with the Lord and talking to him face-to-face. I knew exactly what it was, but sometimes I tend to overthink when nothing is wrong at all. This time, something was wrong. I was off because I recently lost a dear friend of mine who was my godmother in high school. I will not go into detail, but the story is that life's pain consumed her it and it was too much for her to carry on her own. I wish I could have sent her a loving Facebook message like she tends to send me on my sad days. Death is never an easy thing to deal with. She was also a track star back in her days. In my hometown, people inquired about her being my biological mother because we looked so much alike. She polished my nails after school then fed me dinner. Oh, how I am going to miss my friend who was one of the most loyal and honest people I have ever met in my life of twenty-six years old. I know you know my pain, Lord. I guess I should try to get some rest because my flight to Toronto is leaving in the morning and I need to be awake at 3:45am, but I needed this journal time. It was almost forced. I could not go another second without sharing my thoughts. On to the next race! Wait, when I think about it. I have traveled all the world through a sport I had no intention of running after joining the AAU Track Team at the age of twelve. So far, I have traveled to: Trinidad and

Tobago, the Bahamas, Canada, California, Indiana, Missouri, The Cayman Islands, Dominican Republic, Guadeloupe, Colorado, Georgia, Pennsylvania, Michigan, Mississippi, Oregon, Idaho, Iowa, Tennessee, South Carolina, Louisville, Kentucky, Illinois, and now looking to run in Ireland. Not too shabby for a kid who is a product of Palmetto, Florida. God made it happen.

Canada was a sight to see but I was ready to return to the "Sunshine State." The plane lands and I rush to get my belongings from the baggage claim area. I was moving quickly with one thing in mind, I must do this, and it needs to happen now. Although I am terrified, I know God has chosen me to be the one to do this. You can say you forgive a person but deep down in your heart, do you really forgive them? And if you say you forgive them, have you verbally told that person you forgave them. Sometimes the actual offense does not have to be discussed but just letting them know you no longer hold any resentment in your heart, is the true beauty of it all. Who are we to try to condemn others when we continue to do things that may not be pleasing to God daily? Don't mind me, I like to preach to myself sometimes. So, I make the drive to my destination of forgiveness. I sat in the car for a total of ten minutes after rehearsing what to say to this person who has wronged me in the past. Finally, after taking a few deep breathes, I opened the car door, telling myself everything was going to be okay as I approach the front door. For a long time, I believed in monsters but as I got older, I realize that a monster usually hides in the dark. If I could turn the light on and keep that light bright, then the monster has no control over me or my life at this moment. I have been sleeping afraid, in the dark for over fifteen plus years and now is the time to put a stop to it. I walk into the room, and at this point, I do not see this person as a monster anymore. It was different than what expected. I see this person as a regular, imperfect human being who had something inside him years back that compromised his way of thinking. He was not only the monster or person that wronged me, but I looked him in the face for the first time in fifteen years and I can see the hurt. At that moment of heartache, I see that he too was a victim. I thought I was going to murmur these words, "I forgive you," and immediately walk out, but before I knew it, I was pouring my heart out to let this person know how I truly felt. I slowly felt my heart being at ease and my soul at rest. I did it! I mean, God did it! Wait, we did it! I told the individual that God changed me, and God can change anyone if we ask Him to. I told him it is never too late and that I love him. He tried to shake my hand, but I refused and gave him a hug. Talk about one big accomplishment, I felt a heavy load was lifted off my shoulder. That burden I carried for so long is now behind me. I am no longer held captive to the things that tried to destroy me. Today, little Alexis was set free. She turned into a woman today. No longer bound by chains. The mission is now complete. Besides running track and strengthening my spiritual muscles, everything I had experienced was preparing me for this moment. I was fearless, today. I was bold, and God gave me the strength to let go. On the other side is freedom. The freedom that no one else could give me. Now that wound is covered by a big Band-Aid of love. I look forward to competing and running for my life. That is, this new life of freedom that the Lord offers. The race I never ran but longed for.

No Pain, No Gain, Right?

Shortly after running at Penn Relays, I signed a contract to have a track agent represent me for the remainder of the season. The fact that I even have an agent is a blessing. I have not had one since I turned professional in the year 2014. My new agent promised to get me into track meets and take care of whatever was necessary to put me in the best situation possible. So, how do you respond when your agent says he has already submitted and confirmed your name for the 2017 European Circuit and you are expected to fly overseas the following day? This was a surprise to me. I have always had dreams of traveling to Europe. This is exciting news, right? This is what I have been working so hard for, this is the moment I have been waiting for, and it is finally here. My big shot! Besides, in the sport of track and field and almost any sport, you are not guaranteed anything, but a chance and when you get that chance you must take it! No looking back. So, I took a leap of faith. I did not know how this would turn out, but I had a lot to gain and nothing to lose.

A few days passed, and it was closer to the time I would take my month-long trip to Europe. I gave the Chiropractors office notice and then headed home to prepare for traveling. Although I had concerns about living arrangements and such, I proceeded with packing my suitcase. Everything happened so fast and before you know it, I was boarding a flight. Once I arrived, after going through the usual routine at the airport, I settled in my hotel room and changed the television to Law and Order. It did not take me long to realize just how much I take things for granted when I have them readily available to me. I am so grateful for the opportunity and resources I have while living in the United States. Okay, I know you feel a shift in my journal session coming within the next paragraph.

Although the journey has not been easy, I will not give up. I am going to run on to see what the end is going to be. Even at the point of defeat, I remind myself that the battle is not over. Just when I think I am done, I have nothing left, and cannot find the strength I have searched so hard to find, I must go on. I was ready to throw in the towel. Everyone was telling me not to give up, but what am I supposed to do when I am overseas, but still thinking about if my car will be in the driveway when I return home or repossessed, and if I will still have my part-time job at the Chiropractor's office. Talk about stress, trust me, it was on a whole different level.

The summer of 2017 has been one of the most challenging yet rewarding summers of my life. I remember in college when I wanted to study abroad and now I feel like I get a taste of that by competing overseas. I would not be telling the truth if I said it was like a paid vacation because I have been restless since July 10th. It is now July 24th, and I want to go home. After running five track meets in eleven days and moving from hotel to hotel, I kind of miss my old bed. The food is okay, but I am completely off my diet and cannot eat when I want. I am so grateful for the things I have at my leisure at home. It has been a struggle, but I have a hard time complaining because I feel like every great track athlete had to experience this at some point, or maybe not. At the same time, I also know that people are watching. Whether they are watching to see if I give up or persevere, I must continue moving forward. I cannot give someone the satisfaction they do not deserve. Nevertheless, I am here to get the job done. My life story does not involve quitting in any way, shape or form, so I must go on.

Concerning the European Circuit, at times, I do not know how I am going to make it through the next day or race, but that is where I like to brag on my God and how extreme my level of faith is. Faith really is what you cannot see, but it is the very thing you hope for. I think I gave another meaning to having the faith of a mustard seed. My confidence comes from knowing the Lord is always with me and goes before me. If I did not have Him on my side, I would have given up a long time ago. In my darkest times, He has proven Himself to me. Sometimes I get frustrated to the point where I want to scream, but then I quickly realize that is the old Alexis. All in all, I was taught to make the best out what I have, and that is what I have been doing while being overseas.

From track meet to track meet, from different hotels and train stations, I have found a way to let my light shine. That may be half of the purpose for being here. It is a test to see whether I can let my light shine even in unforeseen circumstances. This is not easy, but it never is, so I am willing to do whatever it takes to encourage and inspire someone else. That is where I get revelation when I am feeling down and out. During encouraging someone else, I find myself being blessed. If I have an opportunity to share the gospel while sitting in this small room with three beds, then that is what I am going to do. I know being a witness is bigger than what I am experiencing in the natural. Fear and discouragement are always ahead, waiting to ruin the day, but it is up to us whether we let it get to us or not. Looking out the window of our new hotel, the sky is beautiful, the weather is nice, and I am determined to turn this thing around. Above all, I will send praises now for the victory we (The Lord and I) will celebrate later. This thing is more serious than a sport, it is a battle between believers and nonbelievers. I want everyone to know that God is real.

Success Brings Pain

Forgive me for leaving out the part of my success and redemption. Even in a situation that seems unfair, I got the job done and had some victories. I won a few races and a few bottles of wine, although I am not much of a drinker anymore. I was happy that I could overcome such horrible circumstances, but I was sad at the same time because no one was rejoicing with me. I have not learned of the pain success can bring until now. I am not talking about the growing pains that everyone says I must endure. No one warned me about what comes with success. People change, and friends are no longer supportive. What baffles me is the fact that maybe they were not supportive at all. Yes, I get it, I am a new creation in Christ, so I must forgive them and not repay evil for evil. It is hard to do that in a world so cold. Today was one of those mornings when I wanted to go back to the old me. You know, treat others how they treat me, but soon realized I will only lose. What value does the old Alexis add to my future? I never thought it would be like this. I am in Europe, finally running well, without jet lag, but still dealing with the pressures of life. Success will expose the people you thought were rooting for you. I wonder why we are not taught these things in school when we have job-related courses. It appears they have left out the good parts of what truly matters. No one teaches you how to deal with success after you obtain it and then how to keep it.

Life is an ugly gamble, but I am not willing to gamble my life because it is not my own. Today, I learned, it is easy to go back to the old me. The old me was not pleasing in my Fathers' eyes, but it was there. In fact, the old me is always there, waiting for me to fall. I was so furious today that I scared myself on the inside. It is weird how other people hurt me, but the thought of me hurting them made me sad.

Dear Old Alexis, you cannot take control of me. I left you in the past for a reason. You and I were not working out. You have no place in my future life. The things you have taught

187

me will always be in my subconscious, but I want nothing to do with you. You have caused me more pain than I can bear. You caused me to be hurt, and in return, I hurt others. You showed me the filthy parts of me, and because of that I am determined to be clean, renewed, and set free. You kept me in the dark, and the light could not shine in. You did not know your worth, your standards were low, and you settled. Old Alexis, though you showed me how I did not want to end up in life, I must let you know that you are dead to me. At this point, you serve no purpose. You will not allow me to grow so therefore I must cut all ties, starting with the roots. Anger no longer lives here. Fear has no place in my heart. Defeat is so foreign to me. You did not win. The new Alexis does not acknowledge you in any way, shape, or form. I just buried you, and yes this is goodbye. You will no longer control my life. The thoughts, I take those back. The light overpowers the dark. I know the truth now, and it has set me free from captivity. Pastor Watkins once said something so profound,

"Not everyone in my crowd is in my corner." This includes you, Old Alexis

A Cry for Help

I do not know how much more of this I can take. I won a few races but now I am mentally, emotionally, and physically drained. I wake up and do not know what time of the day it is. Lord, I have been through a lot but never anything like this. I feel like being strong is a blessing and a curse because I have kept this incident to myself for almost a month now. I thought traveling to Europe to compete on a circuit would be a dream come true. How could someone rob me of that? The lesson learned, not everyone who says, "I want to help you," means it. I have also learned that manipulation and deceit are always present in those who seek to do wrong. I am broken internally because I feel as though I am too nice, at times. A person will smile in your face then turn around and stab you in the back, not once but twice just to make sure you are dead. It's a cold world. *Lord, help me guard my heart so it does not turn cold. Lord, you know what it took for me to get here. Lord, I shouldn't ask you, but I am asking, how did I not see this coming before I made the decision to travel here?* My gut was telling me something was wrong. There is no way I can tell my family and close friends the trip I was so excited to take has become a disaster. I cannot tell them I have not had a stable place to lay my head outside of meet arrangements. Sometimes I only eat once a day because the supermarket is far from the hotel. I get here and had to carry my luggage from city to city walking miles to a hotel I thought we would never reach. I have never been so appreciative of a car, train, or bus ride. I have never missed sleeping in my bed more than I do now. I am changing hotels every other day, literally not knowing where I am going to lay my head. All of this because someone I trusted did not keep their word. I almost gave up. The devil thought he had me, but my story does not involve giving up. DeAngelo Williams once said, "Never mix business with morals." At first, I did not understand his logic, but now I do. I cannot let one encounter with a business person corrupt my spirit. I must respond in a businesslike manner. That was the best advice I could have received at this point in my life.

I was also told that if you are not on the Diamond League circuit, this was expected. The Diamond League is where the big dogs are, and "top dollars" are. If I ever needed motivation that was enough for me. I had always dealt with chaos, mistrust, and adversity, so when I am faced with such things, it does not move me. I say that not with pride but with confusion. I have no idea of when I am returning to the United Stated but I must conclude that even if you were to do your research, background check, or what have you, the Devil does wear Prada. Not a direct jab at the label brand itself, but I am simply stating this, a person with malicious intent can only hide behind the mask for so long until the horns show. The first time I get sight of those horns, I am going to stand my ground. Fool me once, no, you will not fool me. I am smarter than the things that have attacked me in the past. I too was once in the dark, and I know how one operates in the dark concerning their actions. So, you must be on guard, stay two steps ahead of the enemy because at every chance, he will try to trip you up. Honestly, the grace of God is what keeps me. Every day is the same. Dark, gloomy, and not knowing where to lay my head or when I will get a hot meal. After being on a strict diet for three years, I am now in Europe eating Domino's pizza and barbecue wings for breakfast. Per the representative, the meal is supposed to last me until the next day. I would like to say this was all a joke, but it is not.

To be honest, I start my day with God in hopes that maybe, just maybe I will have enough strength to get through this day. Now I understand why God says do not worry about tomorrow because tomorrow has its own troubles. That is a true statement indeed. The song "I could only imagine," by MercyMe is giving me peace. This trip has made me realize I have so much more in life to learn. People, places, and things-- three simple nouns we learned in elementary school. I would have never thought it would have such an impact on my life. "It is temporary, soon it will all be over," said a friend of mine. True, but if only I could define the meaning of soon. I guess that is somewhat how God operates also. He does not say when, but He does keep His promises. It is hard to continue to be a light in a dark world. I have learned to only put my trust in God and not people, regardless of what they say. People will always let you down. There have been so many ups and downs on this one trip alone but again, I will fight until the end.

Regardless of my circumstances, I was ready to compete. I arrived at the track in Antwerp, Belgium. Nothing was out of place, and I stuck to the routine. Wake up, pray, read my daily devotional, eat breakfast then get ready to run. I started my warm up which usually consists of six strides down a lane of about fifty meters. Something was different, there was a pain in my left foot I have never felt before. I tried to ignore it as I finished the other runs, but it was impossible. I could not put force into the ground. I walked over to the physio station to see the doctor on duty. They looked at me and said these words, "It could be plantar fascia or a small stressful fracture." She said it was no way to tell for sure without an X-ray. Of course, the doctor said she could not advise me on whether I should run but I should do what I feel is best. So here I am, in Antwerp, Belgium, a long way from home trying to make an executive decision on my own. Talk about pressure! Luckily, the doctor was so kind to let me use her phone and thank God, I could speak with my coach. After going over logistics and details, we concluded that it is too risky to run and possibly make the new injury worse. Although it was the hardest thing to do, I agreed. Part of me still wanted to run, so I tried my best, got in the starting blocks, the gun sounded, but I was not able to finish. At times, I think I am too strong for my own good. The one question an athlete must answer is: How does my body feel and am I pushing it too far? A simple question that requires you to be in sync with your mind and body. As a professional athlete, we are trained to push our body to the limit and beyond. But how do you know when enough is enough and how do you know when you are overworked? That is the term the doctor used, she informed me that my foot was overworked from too much walking and obviously running. To be frank, this whole entire trip does not make sense. From beginning to end, it was filled with test after test, trial after trial. However, I am proud of myself. I did not break or bend but only became more durable, stronger. You get the point. I was built to last. I am concerned about my foot, but I will not let it consume me.

Another day closer to returning to the states and I could not be happier! That probably explains why I have been awake since 6am. Well, besides the fact that I stayed up late planning my weekly goals. A verse comes to mind, no pain is pleasurable at the time, but in the end, it serves its purpose. I had to go through this. It made me stronger and more alert than ever. I am glad to know that nothing and I mean nothing, can break me. Yesterday was very rewarding. I spent time listening to Hope International's livestream message and boy was it on time. The message was titled, "Run with Hope." When Pastor Tony started the message with, "Do not quit," I knew I was going to be blessed, no doubt about it! No matter what I am going through this day, week or month, my season does not end here. There will always be a new season. Quitting for me has never been an option, and it will not be in the future. I was looking forward to next season. Each year, something that I have experienced in the previous season gives me fuel to go harder the following year.

Everyone says be content with what you have. Not a bad statement, however, content can bring mediocrity, and I am striving to be everything but that. As I sit by the window in the hotel lobby, I can easily worry about the challenges of life, but today I am choosing happiness. I will not be discouraged because I have more bills than money. I know what to do to generate income, and that is what I will focus on this week. In the past, I used to dwell on what I did not have and make my problems bigger than my God. At the time, I did not have the wisdom or knowledge to know I had it all wrong. I used to plan every detail of my life, not knowing that even with planning there will be unplanned times, sometimes good and other times bad but one thing remains the same; God is always the same, unchangeable. I am glad God placed people in my life to remind me that I am never alone. One of my dad's favorite sayings, "In spite of." He says with that statement you can put anything before or after it. What a clever man. Who knew, years later, I would be so close to my earthly father and Heavenly Father. Who knew I would make it this far? It is 7am and I am sitting at a breakfast table in Europe, writing one of many books. Although I feel like I am living in a wicked world, I can still see the light in certain people. The light they try to hide and keep inside as if there is no God but look to me and realize they only hurt because of their guard. The word says to guard your heart, but we go to the extent of picking and choosing what we should hide. We let inside what needs to be cast out and put out what does not need to be exposed. In this society, we share more negativity than positivity. How can one survive off such energy?

In my personal life, I have made it my business to not give time to negative things whether it is past, present, or future. I do not perceive my failures as a lost. I am not bitter, and I do not hold on to baggage. You too should practice this model. Life is too short to be anything but happy and allow someone to have power over you. You deserve to be happy. I can tell you from personal experience, God will restore your broken places. Often, we get so caught up in the whys of life instead of just living the good life. As I look forward to this last day in Leuven, Belgium I must remember to forget what is behind and reach forward to what is ahead, pursue my goal, the prize promised by God's heavenly calling. I will have a good attitude no matter what. As disappointed and upset as I would like to be, my heart is changed forever. I will not look to vindicate them who have persecuted me. I will instead bless my enemies. To be honest, none of this makes sense to me, but I know it is the God in me. I do not understand His ways, but I know they are higher than mine, so I will trust him.

While it may not have been the experience I had hoped for, it was needed. I met some individuals along the way who happened to be just as strong as I was. During the "test, I connected with someone while being overseas. He was an inspiration. I call him Mr. Incredible. Not because I want to date him, but because he was familiar with the situation I was going through. After he shared his life story, I was convinced he was sent to help me pass this test. Although he had everything a professional athlete could want at this age, he was one of the humblest athletes I have met thus far. He was straightforward and saw the world as being black and white. He told me when I approached someone, I need to have the one-time rule, so they will know that I am serious. So, this time, I guess I was wrong, not everyone who sends a message via social media is trying to date me. He told me to be real and stay true to myself no matter what happens. I will not try to figure things out, but this new friend showed me God can send messages and use anyone. It is my job to listen. I need to have discernment of course but listen. All I know is that he is a well-respected individual in his sport and he blessed me with what I needed to know at the time. While this may seem random to you, it was the confirmation I prayed for. I wanted to make sure my heart was in the right place and that I was not wrong.

Life has its way of showing and teaching you things you will not learn in a school setting. It is called experience.

It is called growth. It is called life's lessons.

I have learned that God will allow things to happen, but that does not mean he orchestrated them. Evil is in the world, and no one is exempt from pain. We must let go of the past. He never intended for us to live hurt, upset, and holding grudges. Miracles are real, God is real. Yesterday I watched a movie, 'The Shack.' It was a true eye-opener. Jesus is everything to me. To take my place on the cross means so much to me. He showed me what true love is and taught me how to forgive others. He made me a winner, and a conqueror when I thought I was not qualified. God did not forget about me.

So, what is next? Another European Circuit, some great races, a new journal to crack open, new victories, a prosperous future, perhaps a Shoe Sponsorship and many more exciting things. By no means at all am I trying to convince you to do anything. After all, we are given the choice of free will, right? I encourage you to share your story, write your thoughts on paper. Be everything you were created to be. Whatever you decide to do, know this, you are a conqueror in Him. Your past does not define you. Once you get over the feeling of fear which is not real by the way, you will begin to tap into a gift you never knew was there. You will discover your purpose of life and why you were put on this earth. Let's be honest, how many times have you sat and wondered about what your sole purpose on earth and what to do with the time you have left? Through sports, track and field was my outlet and you too can fulfill your destiny with whatever outlet you have. Most people are confused about where to start their journey, but I say, start now. In a race, there is only one winner. We must train in a way to obtain the prize (1 Corinthians 9:24). It is your personal race of life. No one or thing can hold you back. The victory is yours, but first, you must deal with those things which are holding you back from reaching your full potential.

Please remember step one: it starts in the mind. You must make up in your mind that you want better. Step 2: decide what or who your Goliath is. The third and final step: know that whatever you need to be victorious is already in you. In fact, it was given to you at birth. Though this is not an ordinary novel, journal, or diary, I have typed these love-filled words just for you. The winner, the overcomer, the redeemed one. Whoever said you only get one chance in life clearly has not met the Creator. Try Him for yourself. I tried him in my deepest, darkest time and while I may have thought I was in the dark, He was always there. A calm, still, small voice waiting to rescue me. A love I was searching for my whole life since the age of four. A peace I longed for since the age of fourteen. The intimacy I needed at the age of twenty-four. He is the piece to the puzzle I could not complete on my own. Who knew that a story of pain, purpose, and passion would end with a beautiful love story?

He had a plan this whole time. He held me in the palm of His hands and took care of me. When I did not believe in a higher power, He made me a believer. When I wanted to give up on life, He gave me a new life, a fresh start. You can experience this love also. As you draw close to God, He will teach you His ways and strength. I was once confused about the whole "Christ thing" too. I thought I had to be perfect to receive forgiveness and give my life to Him. In fact, I was saved at the age of 21, in college, still partying, drinking, and sinning like it was going out of style.

Trust me, if He can save me, He can save you. Romans 10:9 *"If you declare with your mouth, Jesus is Lord, and believe in your heart that God raised him from the dead, you will be saved."* Yes, I know this is only the beginning, but it all starts with you. It is never too late. If you look at my life story, you will see that anything is possible, but there is no way I made it this far on my own. God has me in the palm of His hand. From a lost little girl looking for love, being a lost soul and trying to escape suicide, to being on the road to redemption, He has made me a believer. There were times when I was forced to take short breaks from typing these words because I could not believe what had happened to me. Now, older, wiser, stronger, and better, I can be fearless and face life head-on. The joy I have in knowing I do not have to do it alone!! In fact, God's grace was already available to me at birth. He was in the abortion clinic with my mom, He was with me when the monster tried to get me, He was with me when I first stepped foot on the track running with the Manatee Mustangs, He was with me when I made all those mistakes at Palmetto High School, and He was with me the nights I cried myself to sleep at Murray State University. He was with me when I walked across the stage to graduate and did not have a clear plan, He protected me in Dallas when I had no place to sleep, He provided for me when I moved back to Florida, and this year, He was with me when I put on the USA Team Uniform to represent our country for the first time. With tears in my eyes, *Lord I thank You. I thank You for not giving up on me. I thank You for always giving me second and third chances. If I had a thousand tongues to say thank you, it still would not be enough. I do not deserve Your love, but You continue to love me unconditionally. You loved me when I did not love myself. You kept me here for a purpose. You showed me that my life mattered to You. I will never know why You did it. The way You allowed me to keep my journals after all these years. Lord, You always had a plan. You were looking down on me, little Alexis, sitting on the floor with her pink diary. You held that key for me until it was time to open that book. You showed me exactly what You wanted this book to say. Even now, I know it is You who is sitting at the computer with me, giving me the strength to type over 60,000 words. You showed me that I did not have to be the smartest in the class to write a book. Faith of a mustard seed is all I needed. You showed me which way to go. You gave me the knowledge and wisdom to do this work for Your kingdom. You knew that someday I would tell my story to make Your name great. You knew exactly where I would be today. Thank You forever for saving me! —Your Beloved Daughter, Alexis*

Like a race, the warm-up prepares you for what is to come that day. In this case, life is a race that you must condition for each day; but please note: at any given time, the unexpected can happen. Life can throw curve balls, but you do not have to take that hit. You may lose a few battles but what matters most is how you respond to adversity. Will you fight back, or will you fold under pressure?

Before turning the next page, I want you to make a declaration, right now, right here.

I _____ WILL NOT GIVE UP. I WILL STAND TALL, FIGHT BACK AND BE STRONG. I CANNOT AND WILL NOT LOSE IN THIS RACE OF LIFE.

TODAY'S DATE:

If I could summarize my life story up until this point, it would simply be this: respect my process. It is true, it is worth it, and it is created especially for you. I look forward to sharing the next set of journal entries with you as I go into full detail about the process on my way to the next Olympics!

"WHEN THE STUDENT IS READY, THE TEACHER WILL APPEAR" – DR. MERIANOS

Acknowledgements

It wasn't until August 2015 that I realized I was writing my life story. Somehow, I had mustered up the courage to share it with the world. I intend to help as many people as possible by writing my journey on paper. Sometimes, it is hard to see the light at the end of the tunnel when you have been working towards a goal for so long, but the journey has been worth it. I have walked this path, but I cannot take full credit. People were strategically placed in my life to help me get where I am today, and for that I am grateful. I would like to thank everyone who has impacted my life and took part in my story. First, I want to thank God for making this dream a reality, my grandmother, Dora Goff, who raised me to be the woman I am today, my mom, Jacqueline Anderson, who is my number one fan, my dad, Anthony Love Sr., who is, and always will be, my best friend and biggest supporter. I also want to thank my soldiers that are always ready for battle, my sisters (Keyuna, Ashley, Angela, and Cardiena) and brothers (Courtney Anderson Sr. and Anthony Love Jr).

I wish to express my sincere thanks to Carolyn Moyer, Trisha Lynn, Jim DeGroot, Gene and Jana Fitch, Coach Robert Kelly, Coach Rod Martin, Coach Tonja McKinney, Curtis Johnson Sr., Curtis Johnson Jr., Coach Jenny Severns, Coach Keisler, Coach Dennis Mitchell, Damu Cherry, Dr. Paul Sorchy, Pastor Tony McCoy, Pastor Roosevelt Watkins, Pastor Allen, Megan Mitchell, Professor Merianos, and my Life Coach, Ashley Camblin.

I am extremely grateful for the people I have met along the way too, you know who you are. This success of mine would not have been possible without you.

ABOUT THE AUTHOR

Alexis Love is a Team USA Track and Field athlete who is currently training full-time to become the fastest woman in the world. She was born and raised in Palmetto, Florida.

After graduating Palmetto High School, Alexis went on to attend Murray State University on a full-ride track scholarship. While attending Murray State, she broke numerous records and earned her spot to compete at the 2012 U.S. Olympic Trials. In 2016, she ran in her second U.S. Olympic Trials.

After walking some very troubling roads, some have named her Resiliency Analyst because of her strong will and determination to accomplish her goals. Alexis also earned her Bachelor's degree in Criminal Justice and is considered a premier alumna. On top of running, Alexis is also an avid journal writer and reader. She is pleased to have published her first self-help book, "Running for My Life, *The Diary of Alexis Love*." Alexis also enjoys being a mentor, serving in her community, modeling, and being a motivational speaker. Alexis Love is a woman of virtue. She is on a mission to impact the lives of millions by spreading love to the unloved.

You can learn more about the author at www.motivatewithlove.com

Made in the USA
Monee, IL
26 April 2023